The Way Knows
Trusting Divine Orchestration

Why Purity Matters as We Evolve

Written By:
Jesse J. Jacoby

Soulspire Publishing
Truckee, CA, 96161

ISBN: 979-8-9900273-6-7
Library of Congress Control Number: 2012921011
Dewey CIP: 641.563   **OCLC:** 213839254

Cover art, font, and layout are all original art by:

Wholesalers to book trade: Nelson's Books and Ingram
Available through Amazon.com, BarnesAndNoble.com

Soul Cannot Be Plagiarized

Expression is soul emanation. Concepts, ideas, and shared thoughts are often misrepresented and regurgitated, yet all translation is borrowed from Source. True originality is not ownership but stewardship – an offering made through energetic channels from muses and guides who choose not to exist in the physical realms.

When words we have spoken or written are echoed elsewhere without consent, we must thank the Source from which they were gifted. Ideas belong to the ether, passing through us like the wind through trees, shaping us but never confined by us. The only claim we hold is how authentically we bring them into form.

We can be inspired by others to find our craft, our dharma, our passion, yet the path is ours alone. Influence is not meant to be replicated but refined, used as a guide to uncover our own resonance rather than to mimic another's sound.

Whether through painting, music, movement, writing, or the countless ways we invoke the artist within, our charge is to remain true. Authenticity is the thread that binds spirit with creation, the invisible signature of the soul woven into all that we express.

Creativity is not imitation – but is remembering. The act of listening deeply, of summoning what is waiting to be born through us, of aligning with the greater orchestration of existence.

The soul's expression cannot be plagiarized because this is beyond ownership; the breath of the infinite, ever-expanding, ever-evolving, uniquely manifest through each who has

.

Arcane Oath: A Call to Divine Protection

I accept my power back. No diversion shall shake me, no illusion shall lead me astray. The universe moves for me, flows through me, and aligns with my will and vision.

My moral compass is too refined to be deceived by false prophets, too attuned to be swayed by ulterior motives cloaked in light. I fortify my angelic forces, shielding them from shadows that dare trespass against my sovereignty.

I stand enshrined in divine protection, bathed in the radiance of celestial guardians who walk beside me. I am intolerant to nonsense, unshaken by dishonesty, immune to deception's whispers. I accept the cosmic orchestration of every experience, every encounter, knowing that even the winds that try to bend me are only shaping my ascent.

I am empowered by everything. Nothing diminishes me. I am free. Unbound by struggle, untouched by hardship, unshackled from all forms of oppression. I am eternally liberated – no chains, no binds, no limits upon my mind or soul.

I call upon my muses, and they come to me, enchanted by the purity of my essence. I invoke clever words to pour from my lips like poetry, to weave their way into the heart of the one who captivates me. May she feel, in every organ, in every cell, that she is cherished, adored, and held.

For love moves through me as freely as the galaxies, and the universe works for me.

Compass of Knowing

Opening Invocation – 15

The Threshold of Knowing - 16

Introduction – The Path to Divine Orchestration - 18

Why Purity Matters - 21

Circling Up - 24

The 1st Realm: Mastering Self - 26

Lesson I: Disciplining the Mind - 27

- *Impress With Intellect* - 30
- *Ascending Levels of Consciousness* - 31
- *Ending the War Within* - 33
- *Treat Your Organs Sacred* - 34
- *Cellular Receptivity* - 36
- *Eating Consciousness* - 37
- *Generational Degeneration* - 38
- *Eat Pure to Think Clear* - 39

Lesson II: Training Your Breath - 44

- *Sacred Breath* - 45
- *Oxygen Is the Life Force of Renewal* - 47
- *Activating the Sacred Blueprint* – 48
- *Mindful Breathing Techniques* - 50

Lesson III: Restoring Fluidity in the Body – 54

- *Learning From Nature's Divine Fluidity* - 55
- *The Body's Sacred Waters* - 56
- *Cessation of Stagnation* - 58
- *Purification & Nourishment of the Body's Fluids* - 59
- *Restoring Flow* - 60

Lesson IV: Microbiome Rebalancing - 64

- *The Microbiome As A Living Organ* - 64
- *Gut Instinct – Can We Really Trust Our Gut?* - 64
- *Gut-Brain Connection & Mental Clarity* – 67
- *Intelligence of the Microbiome* – 67
- *Rewilding Nature's Intelligence* - 68
- *Plant-Based Potency* - 69

+ *Eat Colorful Foods – 70*
+ *Factors the Disrupt Microbial Balance – 72*
+ *Purification & Rebalancing Strategies – 72*
+ *The Microbiome as A Spiritual Gateway - 74*

The 2nd Realm: Aligning with Divine Orchestration - 77

Lesson V: Strengthening Source Connection - 78

+ *God Is All Around - 79*
+ *How We Pray - 80*
+ *Prayer for Awareness - 82*
+ *Spiritual Sorcery - 83*
+ *Keeping the Sacred - 85*
+ *Mantras: A Pathway to Source - 86*
+ *Nourish With Cosmic Rays - 87*
+ *Listen to Spirit - 88*
+ *God Is Within: Strengthening Source Connection - 89*

Lesson VI: Staying Out of Your Own Way - 94

+ *Abstain From Glamorization - 95*
+ *Raise Your Average - 96*
+ *Germinate the Seeds of Your Identity - 97*
+ *Obstructing the Obstacles - 99*
+ *Tame Your Demons - 100*
+ *Call In Angels - 101*
+ *Clearing the Path to Freedom - 102*
+ *Reclaiming Inner Authority - 103*
+ *Surrendering to the Flow - 104*
+ *Reminder to Self - 105*
+ *The Illusion of Superiority - 107*
+ *Eluding Patterns - 108*

Lesson VII: Trusting Divine Orchestration - 112

+ *Being Unafraid - 113*
+ *Merlin's Magic - 115*
+ *Revivification of Magic - 116*
+ *Visual Dysbiosis – Disconnection from Sight - 118*
+ *Regenerating Wholeness – Return to Sovereignty - 119*

The 3ʳᵈ Realm: Living in Integrity - 125
Integrity – The Law of Circulation - 126

Lesson VIII: Embodying Integrity - 127
- ◆ *Walking the Integral Path - 128*
- ◆ *Give What You Need - 131*
- ◆ *Respect the Work - 132*
- ◆ *Wash Yourself of Yourself - 133*
- ◆ *Create the Standard - 134*
- ◆ *Honest Virtues - 135*
- ◆ *Strength of Man – 136*
- ◆ *Give Them Reasons - 137*
- ◆ *Be Non-Conformist - 138*
- ◆ *The Grace of Humility - 139*
- ◆ *The Fortitude of Morale - 140*

Lesson IX: Showing Your Children a Good Way - 147
- ◆ *Move Slow - 150*
- ◆ *Revering Precious Moments in Parenting - 151*
- ◆ *A Child's Requirements - 152*
- ◆ *Dad's Matter - 153*
- ◆ *Sweet Child – A Message for the Next Generation - 155*
- ◆ *Ode to Mothers – Honoring the Givers of Life - 157*
- ◆ *Great Teachers – Embodying Lessons We Share - 158*
- ◆ *The Cosmic Dandelion – Planting Goodness - 159*
- ◆ *Art & Power of Play – Keeping Spirit Alive - 160*
- ◆ *Lions Gate Love – Honoring A Child's Milestones - 162*
- ◆ *Protect What You Love - 163*
- ◆ *The Vastness of Pretty – Holding Reverence - 164*
- ◆ *See God in Others – Honoring the Divine - 165*

Lesson X: Being a Good Person - 174
- ◆ *Reciprocity Is in the Giving – 176*
- ◆ *Choose Ideal Idols – The Power of Influence - 178*
- ◆ *Weaponization of Decency – Restoring Integrity – 180*
- ◆ *Do Not Engage in Divisive Rhetoric - 182*
- ◆ *Ascend Through Humbleness - 183*

Lesson XI: Committing As a Loyal Lover - 191
- *Overcoming Mistakes with Humility & Sincerity – 193*
- *Courageous Love – The Art of Risk & Surrender – 194*
- *Sacred Devotion – Fidelity as an Act of Worship – 195*
- *The Sacred Art of Showing Up – 196*
- *Honoring the Feminine Divine – 197*
- *Transmuting Heartbreak – Returning to Purity - 198*

The 4th Realm: Unifying with Spirit - 203

Lesson XII: Choosing Spirit to Remain Centered - 204
- *Reindigenization – Restoring Sacred Balance – 206*
- *Native Lineage – Reconnecting Wisdom – 207*
- *Aid From Our Ancestors – 209*
- *Redefining Culture – 210*
- *Walking the Path – Embodying Light - 211*
- *Taming Demons – Alchemizing Darkness – 212*
- *Artisan's Hands: Bridge of Spirit & Creation - 213*
- *The Power of Stillness in Turbulent Times – 214*
- *Five Ways to Remain Still & Centered – 215*
- *Breaking Cycles: Eluding Patterns of Scarcity – 216*
- *Oneness: The Illusion of Separation – 217*
- *The Myth of Human Supremacy – 217*
- *Polarity of Creation – 219*
- *Wholeness of Spirit: Returning to Fullness - 220*

Lesson XIII: Respecting the Spirit of Nature - 224
- *Fractals of Abundance - 226*
- *Put the Machines to Sleep: Honoring Spirit - 227*
- *Forest Kinship – Ancient Teachers of the Wild - 229*
- *Wisdom From Wind: Breath of Nature's Spirit - 233*
- *Kidneys of Earth: Vital Connections - 235*
- *Snake Medicine – Transforming Fear - 238*
- *The Honorable Harvest - 239*

Author's Epilogue – Become A Vessel for the Way - 244
- *One Day - 246*

Note To My Children: A Legacy of Wisdom - 248

Opening Invocation

Thank you, divine guides, for placing trust in me, for choosing me to walk this path, for shaping me into the one who listens, who learns, and who leads. I offer gratitude for showing me how to balance unshakable masculine strength with flowing feminine grace, for allowing me to wield power with softness, to walk with certainty and still be moved by the wind.

Thank you for reminding me that my temperament is my own to govern, that no storm within me is greater than my ability to return to calm. Thank you for the breath, the anchor, the rhythm that always calls me back. Each moment of disharmony is an invitation — a request from the universe to hydrate, to open my hips, to realign with my center, to breathe deeper into the spaces where tension hides.

I am grateful beyond words for the wisdom that flows through me, for the knowledge that finds me at dawn and lingers in the twilight, shaping my teachings, weaving into the fabric of my writings, pouring forth into every encounter.

The work is real. The years spent leading shadows to light, standing firm in the face of adversity, refusing to break under the weight of my trials – these moments have forged me. They have not shattered me; they have sculpted me into a more noble man.

Thank you for instilling within me impenetrable discipline, the necessary foundation upon which I may continue to decipher codes of existence, to read the messages written in the unseen. My prayer is to melt away all misalignments so I may walk wholly in my center. To dissolve distortions and incinerate incongruencies, so that integrity is not merely a virtue, but my nature.

I call in the abundance that is mine by divine right. I welcome the love that has been chosen for me by divine selection. I invoke sacred reciprocity in all my relations – with my children, in partnership, in my work, in my offerings, in the goodness I cultivate and receive. May we all find the courage to step out of our own way, and to surrender resistance, so that we may be redirected onto our path with clarity and grace.

The Threshold of Knowing

You are not here by accident. This book found you because a deeper part of you is ready to remember.

There is a current running through your life, ancient and unseen. This stream has whispered during intervals of stillness, tugged at you in moments of doubt, and pulled you back onto your path when you wandered too far. *The Way Knows* is an eternal verity encoded in your breath, your blood, your bones.

To walk this way is to surrender to a greater intelligence – one that does not rush, does not scream, but waits in quiet certainty for your willingness to listen. The whisper you await, what your spirit strains to hear, is the voice that speaks through wind, through instinct, through wisdom of your body when the mind is too loud.

This is not a book of answers, but a book of realignment. A key to remembering. Here, you will not be asked to become someone new, but to return to who you have always been. You will uncover the divine within, not chase. You will place reverence before ambition, integrity before illusion, and alignment before achievement.

You were born to embody your path, not chase after a vision that was engineered. Every experience, every wound, every sacred encounter has shaped you for this moment. You are not late. You are not lost. You are precisely where the Great Intelligence placed you to remember your origin and reclaim your power.

This book is a mirror, not a map. As you navigate through these pages, may you not simply read the words, but *feel them* rearrange you. Let what is dormant rise and what is false fall away. Allow the knowing to return – not through force, but through quiet recognition. The way does not scream. The way simply *knows.*

So, take a breath. Feel your weight in the chair, your spine, your pulse, your presence. You are stepping into sacred ground. This is the beginning of your return.

Introduction – Path to Divine Orchestration

"Be like a hollow bamboo, empty and receptive, and the divine will flow through you." – Paramahansa Yogananda

The Way Knows is not merely a phrase; but is an understanding – an acknowledgment of the cosmic rhythm guiding us beyond the constraints of conditioned reality. To know *The Way* is to trust in divine orchestration, to align with veiled currents of wisdom that flow through existence. This book is a bridge between known and unknown, illuminating a path of remembrance, where we restore the interconnectedness of mind, body, and spirit.

To understand this sacred symbiosis, we must first recognize how deeply fragmented we have become. The pseudo-culture engineered from capitalism, colonialism, corporatism, genocide, and war has fractured our perception, relegating us to cycles of misinformation and illusion. Public education and mass indoctrination impose agendas that bind the mind to a reality carefully curated by unseen architects.

Humanity is led to believe in only five senses, yet within us lie dormant faculties – the sixth and seventh senses – that, once awakened, reveal the intricate web of energy connecting us to all existence. Even the ears, beyond their role in hearing, attune us to the subtle guidance of magnetism, directing us like celestial compasses toward truth.

We are taught to navigate through four directions – east, north, south, and west – and are instructed to draw a square around this compass. But what of the fifth direction? Where does this lead? What revelations await those who dare to seek beyond the mapped territories of convention?

Following forged paths that have been paved for us leads only to destinations already charted. From an early age, we are imprinted with beliefs that condition us to trust those who care for us, assuming they are guiding us with honesty and integrity. Yet, with each passing generation, the wisdom of circular knowledge grows more endangered.

The modern world feeds upon distortions of truth, promoting destructive habits, false histories, and parasitic influences that sever our connection to higher wisdom. This book is an invitation to step away from square knowledge and embrace the wholeness of circular wisdom.

The purity of the body is fundamental to unlocking the full spectrum of human potential. Scientific and spiritual foundations align in this understanding. Disease does not arise from chance but from imbalance – manifested through the saturation of acids, gut dysbiosis, and the infiltration of foreign microbes disrupting the harmony of the microbiome. Just as the body succumbs to toxicity, so too does the mind and spirit when subjected to cultural, educational, and spiritual dysbiosis.

I am on a quest to reclaim my purity that is a divine right. At birth, this was abstracted from me – replaced with simulated interventions: chemicals, artificial lights, synthetic air, and invasive procedures. These were not mere happenstances but deliberate interferences, designed to obstruct my connection with spirit.

I was created to exist as organically as jade vine, untainted and luminous, yet my early existence was met with forces intent on dulling this radiance. Humanity has been subjected to this same plight, our essence obscured by the constructs of confused men who have surrendered their dignity to greed and Wetiko – the force of spiritual corruption that distorts perception.

When we restore purity within the body, we remove the greatest barrier to ascension and limitless potentiality. The spirit is an extension of the unseen, the body a vessel within the physical realm. The two are meant to move in effortless harmony, yet the introduction of toxins – physical, mental, and spiritual – breeds discord. Calcification hardens arteries and joints. Mucoid plaque obstructs intestinal walls, diminishing nutrient absorption and dulling the mind. Nasal congestion stifles spiritual communication, cutting us off from divine inspiration. Abrasive thoughts corrode the psyche, undermining clarity.

To restore our rightful connection, we must cleanse, refine, and attune our essence to the highest expression.

Life itself breathes purity into existence. Elemental essences – offered by algae, fungi, mosses, soil, plants, trees, and all living forces – are ever-present gifts designed to elevate us. They whisper their wisdom through the air we inhale, nourishing us with sacred energy. As we breathe, let us do so with gratitude, for every inhalation is a gift, an offering of alignment with the greater whole.

Witness the conception of light as a hummingbird pollinates an unfurling petal, or as a bee carries golden pollen to the hive where alchemy transforms this sustenance into sweet honey. These miracles occur in simultaneity, weaving the fabric of existence in ways we scarcely comprehend. Yet, the challenge remains – to expand our awareness, to perceive the unseen, to step beyond limitation into divine orchestration.

We pray to one God, yet wage wars in the name of division, debating whose articulation of the Divine is supreme. In Mayan tradition, there are three Gods: The God below, the God all around, and the God above. Why do we confine our prayers to a single plane of existence? Why do we not seek God in the soil beneath our feet, in the breath of the wind that encircles us, and in the celestial expanse above?

We exist within a game of frequency. Understanding this reveals our power to ascend into greater dimensions of being. This book deciphers the codes required for navigating a more meaningful path – one rooted in integrity, discipline, and divine order. These lessons have shaped my own evolution, and I am honored to share them with you. This is more than an offering; this is an invitation to reclaim your divinity, to remember the truth embedded in your being, and to walk The Way that Knows.

Why Purity Matters

"God is not attracted to outer appearances, but rather by the cleanliness of the inner self." – Shirdi Sai Baba

Purity is the threshold to liberation, and a key to unshackling ourselves from burdens of fragmentation, contamination, and distortion. To be pure is to exist in a state of wholeness, free from the weight of corruption that distorts our perception and hinders our evolution. This is the great unfolding of the soul's journey – to experience not only freedom but fulfillment. Is this not the goal of life itself?

Spiritual purity sustains innocence, not as naivety, but as an undiminished clarity that allows light to pass through unfiltered. This can be represented as a foundation of illumination, and redemption of the soul from erroneous ways. When body, mind, and spirit are purified, we create a vessel capable of receiving and transmitting divine wisdom. This attunement grants us a direct and unimpeded connection with Source, where cosmic guidance flows effortlessly. To trust in divine orchestration is to trust that, in the surrender of impurity, we align ourselves with the natural order of existence.

Physical purity is an act of honoring our essence, which is boundless and luminous. This can only be sustained by what is inherently pure – pristine air, untainted water, vibrant living foods, and movement in alignment with rhythms of nature. The external mirrors internal; as we nourish the body, we simultaneously cleanse the soul.

A fragmented mind is a restless mind, undisciplined and chaotic, caught in a ceaseless interchange of impulses and reactions. True silence, the gateway to higher perception, arises when this interchange ceases, when the pendulum of distraction is stilled, never to be set in motion again. Purification is not merely an act but a state of being – one in which limitation, dark habits, and destructive routines dissolve. The path to transcendence is found in the shedding of layers that no longer serve us.

How, then, do we purify in such a way that our spirit merges seamlessly with the spirit of all that is? The answer lies in love. Love, in highest form, seeks out impurity, not to judge, but to transmute. Love, like breath, circulates through us, nourishing every cell and dissolving that which is unnatural. To love is to engage in the alchemy of purification, leaving behind only what is true, authentic, and everlasting.

The *Divine Language of Celestial Correspondences* teaches that the sovereign mind perceives the light that explains the mysteries of life. True knowledge does not merely interpret; but perceives the spiritual essence of all things. To refine our inner faculties is to cultivate this higher perception, to unveil the wisdom embedded in the fabric of existence.

One of the greatest truths I have encountered states: *"If you could forget everything and anticipate nothing, you would automatically find yourself piercing the boundaries that shield you from the perception of a higher reality."* Purity requires this level of surrender – a relinquishing of attachment to past conditioning and future expectations, allowing reality to unfold without distortion.

"The gist of all worship," I was once told, *"is to be pure and do good to others."* To live a truly loving life, we must purify the life we have. Love demands a strength that is both gentle and indomitable. This requires the resilience to forgive, courage to trust, and wisdom to remain unwavering in truth.

Forgiveness requires a quiet strength that cannot be denied. To return to trust after betrayal. To remain honest when faced with deception. To hold one's center when love is not honored. To stand in loyalty when children are denied their right to a father's presence. To fight for love when the world seeks to disentangle the sacred bond of time.

This is an allegiance that does not die, a force that transcends temporal conflicts and unites us in eternal oneness.

Merlin once explained that *"the titanic forces swirling through the cosmos do not war with one another. They are allowed to exist and evolve as part of nature's tendency toward growth."* Likewise, in our relations, we are called to embody this principle – to allow, to accept, and to transmute, rather than to resist and divide. Our responsibility is to remain steady and calm, unwavering in the face of all circumstances.

Purity perfects attention, transforming chaos into order and confusion into clarity. To be pure is to possess the discriminating awareness of compassion, to stand strong in truth without descending into judgment, to embody every virtue in highest form.

Purity is not a restriction, but an expansion. Not an absence; rather a fullness. A liberation, not limitation. To purify is to return to our original brilliance – to be wholly and completely ourselves, merged in divine harmony with all that is. When we begin to see the seeds of opportunity in the ashes of disaster, we know that trust is taking root within us.

Circling Up

A droplet sends ripples through a pond, forming an ever-expanding circle – a reflection of change, growth, and wholeness. The center of the circle evokes Source – unbroken, and infinite. There is no beginning, no end. When we gather in this formation, we are reminded that no one stands above or below another, that every voice is heard, every heart is seen.

Connection resurrects the light within our reflection. We remember who we are in the presence of others who truly see us. In sacred councils, we recall our divine purpose, release burdens we have carried alone, and step into the fullness of our being.

In indigenous cultures, councils are formed in circles so that wisdom flows freely among all. The Sioux say, *Love settles within the circle, embracing each occupant, and thereby lasting forever.* In a world built on lines and hierarchies, where some are placed at the front and others relegated to the back, the circle restores balance. No one is left behind. All are held in remembrance.

Healing happens within community. When we circle up with others who match our frequency, we experience a resonance that cannot be felt in solitude. Energy passes between us, feeding our spirits, and sustaining us. What empowers us is kept. What disempowers us is released.

We arrive in authenticity, unafraid to be vulnerable, willing to shed the masks that no longer serve us. We come ready to witness and be witnessed, to speak truthfully, to move through discomfort rather than formulating reasons to avoid. Within the safety of the circle, we confront our shadows. We acknowledge where we have fallen short – where we have been dishonest, complacent, or afraid. In this sacred space, we take responsibility. This is how we reclaim our sense of belonging.

If we need support, we ask. We voice our struggles and are met with unwavering presence. When we rise from the circle, we do so not as the same people who entered but as those who have embraced change. We walk forward with integrity, embodying the transformation we seek.

Our integrity is not determined solely by what we say, but by what we do after the words have been spoken.

The greatest obstacles in our lives are not placed before us as punishments but as allies in our evolution. Every hardship, every loss, every severed attachment is an invitation to rise. When we let go of past versions of ourselves – those tethered to suffering, victimhood, or regret – we create space to embody who we were always meant to be. Each day, we renew our commitment to growth. We ask ourselves, *what is the story I need to release? What new story will I write?*

We are the architects of our own transformation. The path we walk is ours to choose from and is made easier when we walk together. The strength of brotherhood and sisterhood is in unity – when we unite, when we allow ourselves to be seen, when we open our arms instead of closing our hearts. This is when we heal.

There is an Ethiopian proverb that reminds us, *when spiders unite, they can tie down a lion.* Alone, we may struggle. Together, we overcome. When we are weighed down by doubt, fear, or self-sabotage, we can call upon those who stand beside us. We can gather, share, and exhale. In the presence of our brothers and sisters, we release what no longer serves us. We speak our darkness into the fire, and in return, receive reflections, insights, and reminders of our strength. The weight becomes lighter. The path becomes clearer.

In a community, diversity of experience strengthens us. Each person brings their wisdom, forged through their trials. By listening, learning, and humbling ourselves to the perspectives of others, we expand our understanding. We take what resonates, honor what does not, and move forward, more whole than before.

Connection is the cure. When we are lost, we are disconnected from our source. If we are unwell, we have distanced ourselves from nature's healing. In sacred relationships – with each other, with the Earth, with the divine – we return to balance. To be seen fully, to be received wholly is the medicine we have always needed.

The 1st Realm: Mastering the Self

Lesson I: Disciplining the Mind

"Your worst enemy cannot harm you as much as your own unguarded thoughts." – Dhammapada

The mind is a river, ceaselessly flowing, carrying residuum of our past, debris of distraction, and currents of desire. Left unguarded, thoughts can meander without direction, eroding the banks of discipline and clarity. A trained mind, like a river guided by wise embankments, flows with purpose, carving a path toward wisdom and awakening.

Our inner world is reflected outward. The radiance in our eyes, warmth of our skin, spontaneity of our laughter, and ease of our movements are a testament to harmony of the mind. A mind at peace is expressed through a body that glows with vitality, words that carry grace, and a presence that feels like home.

The mind is not a separate entity from the body, this organ breathes, expands, and contracts like tides. Few realize that the temporal bones of the skull, beveled like gills of a fish, make the brain a primary breathing mechanism. Every inhale is not merely a function of the lungs but a movement of consciousness, a cycle of expansion. Brain respiration, the act of drawing life-giving energy through the meridian system, is the silent force animating our existence. When we engage in conscious breathwork, we are not merely oxygenating the body but inviting prana – the breath of life – into every cell. The purity of this breath dictates the purity of thought, and in turn, the clarity of our perception.

To discipline the mind is to be freed from the tyranny of distraction. In a world saturated with noise, we must learn the art of stillness. Meditation is not an escape but a return – to the self, the breath, and the infinite space within. By centering ourselves in balance, we create a sanctuary where wisdom can arise unimpeded.

Science now affirms what sages have long known: the mind is malleable. Neuroplasticity reveals that focused awareness reshapes neural pathways, strengthening our ability to remain present. Discipline is the sculptor of consciousness.

Through deliberate practice, we hone an ability to dwell fully in the moment, untethered by past regrets or future anxieties. Mind, body, and spirit are not separate entities but an interwoven symphony. When the mind is disciplined, the body follows in health, and spirit in harmony. This lesson is not about control – but is about liberation, about wielding the mind as an instrument of precision rather than a wandering echo of external chaos.

Health is not merely the absence of disease, but the full expression of vitality, the ability to utilize our energy and body according to our conscious intentions. To discipline the mind is to awaken to this essence of concentrated consciousness, to refine our awareness until we are no longer pulled by impulse but moved by presence.

As I once learned, *"Mind is the unemptiable source of phenomena – which requires nothing yet is the ground of everything."* The mind holds the key to unlocking inner happiness, and happiness becomes a shield, making us immune to disturbances from the outer world. Yet, if left untrained, the mind can convert and reshape as an unmoored wind, carrying us in circles, eroding balance, and scattering our awareness.

To discipline the mind is to cease unnecessary battles within, to refuse the invitation to struggle, and to reclaim our attention from the chaos of distractions. We can receive this as a form of self-respect, a refusal to misappropriate our energy by entertaining illusions that do not serve us. When thoughts no longer chase each other like echoes in a hollow chamber, a great silence emerges. A cosmic pause, or celestial calm, in which the soul speaks.

To meditate is to immerse oneself fully in Spirit. This is the highest calling of the mind, the most profound act of balance, and the surest way to align with divine guidance. In stillness, scattered fragments of thought coalesce into clarity, and simple truths of the universe unfold before us. We are invited to relax in every situation, to release the reflex of overreaction, and to loosen the knots of emotional entanglement without summoning the stern bureaucracy of judgment.

How do we move with the rhythm of life without being enslaved by tides of success and failure, or gain and loss? The answer is restraint without repression, discipline without rigidity – an unwavering equanimity that remains whole, whether the moment brings abundance or emptiness.

Perhaps clarity begins the moment we recognize our patterns of distraction as they arise, choosing, again and again, to return to presence. Why drag the baggage of past experiences into each fresh moment, when we could meet life anew with an open, unburdened mind? Maybe the firmest ground we will ever stand on is the willingness to embrace the unknown, to make peace with uncertainty – to let insecurity become our greatest security.

In stillness, we discover a silent force that weaves the fabric of reality. In presence, we become aligned with the orchestration of the cosmos. When we cease striving, life conspires in our favor. Our slightest whisper sends ripples through the ethereal, calling forth fulfillment of our truest desires.

Every seeker must learn the art of concentration – to build unseen temples within, to recognize the divine in every face, and to see God's quiet smile reflected in their own.

To master the mind is to master one's path. This is the first step in aligning with *The Way that Knows*.

Impress with Intellect

"Raise your words, not voice. Rain grows flowers, not thunder."

Wisdom is not measured in how loud we speak but in the depth of our words. Chief Red Eagle once taught that *angry people want us to see their power, but loving people help us to embrace our own.* The way we express ourselves defines the level of our evolution. Each word is a stone laid upon the path of our ascension.

Acuity and brilliance emit a frequency that is alluring. To rewrite narratives in this world we are required to raise our words. Knowledge is a missing ingredient that even schools lack. The information most men digest is formulated without ethics. There are no morals in today's stories. Our values have been displaced with measures of dollars. Material things have no merit. Frugality is more worthy of praise.

Merlin's guidance was to seek wisdom where still present: *"Find gold in old books and dig up treasures in verses and lines. Do not go after what plagues the mortal kind."* He advised, *"Never compete with fools. Focus on elevating your intelligence, expanding your vocabulary, and broadening your mind".* He taught me the true wealth of articulation: *"Be rich with eloquence and spend your fortunes in how you speak. Emanate grace each time you open your mouth, let grandeur echo in your voice when you sing."* Most importantly, he instilled in me a purpose: *"Use your vocals to influence the change we all seek. Encourage others to embrace being unique and go after what is distinct."*

Language is a force, a manifestation of consciousness. To elevate our vocabulary is to elevate our being. When confusion or rage clouds the mind, let us transmute these emotions into blossoming flowers of wisdom. Knowledge is a treasure that lies beyond the reach of fools; to unearth this luminous pearl requires devotion, patience, and clarity.

Real power is found not in force, but in articulation. Be rich in eloquence. Let your words shape reality with intention. In a world of noise, let your voice carry meaning. This is how we impress – not by volume, but with intellect.

Ascending Levels of Consciousness

"Molecules dissolve and pass away, but consciousness survives the death of the matter on which she rides." – Merlin

As the current of energy flowing through us increases, so too does the scope of our awareness. Consciousness is not static – this is an unfolding, an ever-expanding horizon that stretches beyond the architecture of the tangible. We pass through sacred thresholds on this journey, each being a bridge between who we were and who we are becoming.

Growth can be defined as a measure of our awakening. Happiness is not found in external possessions but in the realization that we are evolving, shedding old layers, and stepping into greater clarity. Wisdom – the highest attainment – is not merely knowledge amassed but the ability to embody truth with grace, carry stillness within movement, and listen as deeply as one speaks.

These are the five levels of consciousness we experience as we transcend and evolve through life. They are gateways that invite us to expand, refine, and transcend. Some will resist the call, gripping tightly to the comfort of illusion, while others will rise, drawn by an inner knowing that there is more beyond the visible. To move through these levels is not a race but a remembrance, a return to the essence of what has always been within.

The Dormant State – The lowest level of consciousness, where awareness is veiled by conditioning and illusion. One is guided by impulse, trapped in reactionary patterns, unaware of greater forces at play. Here, the ego reigns supreme, seeking gratification over truth.

The Awakening – A stirring occurs within. The individual begins questioning long-held beliefs and recognizes the presence of unseen currents shaping their life. Synchronicities appear, and an urge to seek deeper meaning takes root. This stage is often marked by inner turmoil, as the structures of conditioned reality begin to crack.

The Disciplined Seeker – With newfound clarity, one embarks on the path of mastery. Meditation, mindfulness, and conscious living become priorities. The individual learns to transmute negativity into wisdom, refining thoughts and emotions. They move beyond distraction and cultivate the art of presence.

The Expanding Visionary – Awareness broadens beyond the self. Compassion deepens, and one understands their interconnectedness with all beings. Perception sharpens, allowing the ability to read energy, interpret symbols, and harness intuition. The individual becomes a bridge between realms, walking with wisdom yet remaining grounded in service.

The Luminous Sage – The final threshold of embodied enlightenment. Thought dissolves into pure presence, and all distinctions fade. The individual radiates peace, existing in harmony with cosmic order. They are no longer a seeker but a beacon, guiding others through their mere presence. Here, wisdom is no longer sought – but simply is.

To ascend through these levels is not a race but a return – a remembering of what has always been within. Identify which level has resonance with where you are at now, and work toward embodying the Luminous Sage.

Ending the War Within

" Ending the war inside yourself means bringing the conflict among all your personalities to an end. You can relieve the shadow self of the burden of held energies from the past and thus create a condition for inner peace." – Deepak Chopra, *The Way of the Wizard*

The most profound battles are not fought on fields of war but within corridors of our minds. There is an inner fragmentation, a ceaseless dialogue between the selves we have been and the self we are becoming. Wounds from the past, echoes of old conditioning, and a tug-of-war between ego and essence keep us in a state of perpetual unrest. The way home is directed through silence, stillness, and solitude.

To end internal war is to cease the inner conflict that has divided our consciousness. This requires us to sit with ourselves, to listen deeply, and to understand that our past is not a chain but a teacher. In stillness, we dissolve the need to fight. In silence, we strip away the noise of external influences. In solitude, we meet the unshakable truth of our being.

The integration of the shadow self is not an eradication but an embrace. Every suppressed emotion, every fragmented piece of our psyche, seeks only to be acknowledged, to be held in the light of awareness. By allowing space for these aspects of ourselves, we create conditions for true peace to emerge. Forgiveness, both of self and others, becomes a salve that heals wounds of inner discord.

The path to resolution is not found in seeking validation from the external world but in cultivating harmony within. The secret to returning to our center is the willingness to surrender to presence, self-acceptance, and the great unfolding of divine orchestration.

When the war ends, we do not lose. We gain clarity, serenity, and a renewed connection to *The Way that Knows*.

Treat Your Organs Sacred

The masters teach that *"youth is not a time of life, but a quality, a trait of character, a mental and physical state."* *"Youth"*, they say, *"is not marked by passage of years but by the vitality and resilience of the body"*. *"In youth,"* we are instructed, *"the organs and structures are elastic, pliable, and yielding."* As years pass, rigidity takes hold, arteries thicken, blood supply to our organs diminishes, elasticity is replaced by ossification, senses dull, and vitality begins to wane.

The cause of decrepitude is not time, but rather the choices we make. The air we breathe, land we dwell upon, food we ingest, habits we cultivate, and burdens we bear all shape our longevity or hasten our decline. There is a race toward devitalization. The modern world rewards indulgence in what depletes us, fostering habits that abstract us from our natural state of balance.

Alcohol, processed foods, pharmaceuticals, and tobacco are architects of slow decay, yet their consumption is celebrated, encouraged, and normalized. The subconscious is groomed for self-destruction, much like fungi spore under the right conditions, flourishing in damp and dark corners where light seldom reaches.

I recently dreamt of four friends from my youth. In the dream, they were vibrant and whole, untouched by the addictions that claimed them in waking life. I was ecstatic to see them healthy again, for they had spent their years devitalized, consumed by substances that robbed them of their essence. I tried, in life, to guide them toward vitality – to encourage them to drink clean water, to nourish their bodies, to choose foods that carried the breath of life rather than residuum of chemicals. But my efforts were in vain. I watched them consume their way into an early grave.

These experiences gave me a revelation: I had the same options they did. I walked the same streets, breathed the same air, faced the same temptations. Yet, I chose differently. I honored my organs as sacred vessels. I preserved my ethereal strength. In doing so, I reclaimed my sovereignty.

Each organ in our body is an individual entity, a self-sustaining organism working in harmony with the whole. When one falls out of balance, the others must compensate, adjusting, adapting, laboring to restore equilibrium. When our organs are healthy, we are mentally sharp, emotionally stable, and spiritually attuned. A disciplined mind cannot exist in a body weighed down by toxicity. If we wish to refine our consciousness, we must begin with the temple this intelligence is housed in.

To honor our organs is to honor life. This is an act of devotion, a recognition that within us exists an intricate, intelligent system designed for renewal and longevity. Treat your organs with reverence, and they will serve you with clarity, strength, and life force. Choose pranic energy. Choose life. This, too, is the path of *The Way that Knows.*

Cellular Receptivity

Beneath our skin, within the omniscient flow of our body, lies a network of receptivity, an intricate system designed to read and respond to the natural world. Proprioceptors in our feet adjust our balance, attuning us to the surface beneath us. Walking barefoot across ice or the forest floor, these receptors awaken, sending signals to generate warmth or shift our stance, ensuring harmony with the land. Encased in shoes, this wisdom is silenced, our connection sundered.

Our skin and eyes are lined with photosensitive receptors, known as rhodopsin, that detect shifts in light and temperature. In the sun's embrace, these receptors activate a cascade within our cells, producing melanin, preparing the body for ultraviolet exposure, and strengthening our resilience. Yet, when we veil our eyes with sunglasses and coat our skin with synthetic sunblock, we disrupt this intricate communion, dulling the natural language of our cells.

Our body does not forget. Even when burdened with toxins – processed foods, impure water, artificial stimulants – the innate intelligence we are ordained to in our body seeks restoration. When exposed to nature's elements, the sun and cold, the response is expelling foreign debris and purging what does not belong. We call this sickness, but this is merely the body's wisdom at work, an ancient intelligence seeking equilibrium.

As we cleanse our bodies, nourish them with wholesome foods, drink pure water, and move with the rhythms of Earth, this natural receptivity returns. We remember the necessity of walking barefoot upon the land, allowing the sun's light to touch our skin, and trusting elements to heal rather than harm.

To reside in an attuned body attuned is to reside in a vessel prepared for clarity, balance, and expansion. To honor this sacred receptivity, listen deeply, and move through life with a mind and body in perfect accord is an act of reverence. This, too, is discipline of the mind – the practice of presence, art of connection, and remembrance of what has always been known.

Eating Consciousness

We are encouraged to eat from gardens, not graves. With discipline this can easily be accomplished. The food we consume is not merely fuel; this is intelligence. Every bite carries a frequency, a whisper of cosmic information encoded in the molecular structure of plants. Neutrinos, subatomic messengers born from the heart of stars, rain upon the Earth, infusing all living matter with subtle imprints of celestial wisdom. When we ingest plants that have bathed in this energy, we inherit the messages they hold.

Raw, living foods – vibrant greens, ripened fruits, mineral-rich roots – carry the pulse of life. Their phytonutrients, enzymes, and bioactive compounds act as conduits of consciousness, awakening cells, enlivening tissues, and refining our awareness. Chlorophyll, the green essence of plants, mirrors hemoglobin in blood, enhancing oxygenation and detoxification – a direct bridge between sunlight and spirit. Polyphenols, flavonoids, and carotenoids do more than nourish, they illuminate.

Science affirms what sages have long known. The microbiota in our gut, our second brain, thrives on plant fibers and polyphenols, synthesizing neurotransmitters like serotonin and dopamine. The gut-brain axis is a direct channel of consciousness. What we feed ourselves enriches our vitality and mind.

If we consume dead foods – processed, refined, chemically laden – we invite stagnation. These are depleting, not nourishing. They reduce energy, leaving residues that cloud the mind, dampen the spirit, and obstruct the natural flow of vitality. They hinder us from receiving the wisdom encoded in nature's design.

The way forward is simple: eat with reverence. Choose foods that carry light, that hold the memory of the sun, that have absorbed the whispers of wind and nourishment of Earth. Eat not only for sustenance but for illumination. In every meal, there is an opportunity – to align with the intelligence of nature, to fortify the temple of the body, to elevate the consciousness that resides within.

Generational Degeneration

The aptitude and potential of humankind diminishes with each generation, eroded by weakened genetics and hybridized DNA through cellular grafting from the ingestion of animals, environmental toxicity, and the weight of unhealed ancestral traumas. We are not merely inheritors of history but carriers of epigenetic imprints, coded into our biology. Each decision we make – what we eat, how we live, the conditions we accept – either strengthens or weakens the lineage we pass forward.

Once, we lived in sync with the rhythms of Earth, drawing vitality from elements, from fruits of the land, from the wisdom of the sun and soil. But modern civilization has severed this sacred reciprocity. The body, once an adaptive force, now labors under the burden of devitalization. Each generation is raised within a different framework of conditioned dependency – convenience over vitality, indulgence over discipline, ignorance over wisdom. This gradual decline is what I call *generational degeneration*.

When we receive misinformation disguised as knowledge and are raised in artificial environments devoid of natural harmony, our minds become docile, spirits dull, and bodies frail. The food we consume – processed and void of life force – compounds this atrophy, leaving us malnourished, and inept in thought and morality. Intelligence dims, wisdom is obscured, and we drift from the brilliance that once defined our ancestors.

This is a call to realign with what has been lost. To raise a generation not bound by inherited decay but empowered by conscious restoration. Allow your children to eat foods that hold the imprint of the sun, that whisper secrets from trees, that pulse with the electric force of nature's intelligence. Let them run barefoot, absorbing the currents of Earth.

Be mindful of the thoughts you allow to govern your emotions, the influences that shape your perception, and the habits that define the course of your evolution. With every choice, you are either reinforcing the cycles of generational degeneration or reclaiming the vitality that has been lost.

Eat Pure to Think Clear

"The subtle energy of food becomes the subtle energy of your mind."
– Swami Sivananda

Purity is a birthright, yet modern life extracts from our essence. Conditioned to consume impurities, and trained to conform, we gradually lose our innate clarity and wholeness. This purity is not lost. We can reclaim our divine completeness through the choices we make, the foods we eat, and energy we invite into our being. We must eat with intention, welcoming in the consciousness and vibrancy that life offers in the most natural forms.

Eating is more than sustenance. This is an exchange of energy, an alchemy of transformation. When we consume living, nutrient-dense foods, we are not just feeding our bodies, we are elevating our frequency, refining our awareness, and deepening our connection to the intelligence of nature. To eat foods in the process of decay, to consume substances that are unnatural, is to adulterate this sacred communion.

For over a decade, I have thrived on plant-derived foods, selecting only those that nourish rather than deplete. I do not consume alcohol, soy, gluten, or the processed "vegan" staples that often lead to imbalance. I do not heat salt or cook oils, nor do I ingest ingredients that masquerade as nutritious, such as synthetic yeast derivatives. Instead, my diet is rich in raw, unprocessed sustenance – living foods that pulse with life force, that sustain and fortify without compromise.

The reward? I do not experience sickness. My vitality remains intact. This is the tradeoff – a commitment to purity in exchange for a body that remains resilient, a mind that remains clear.

Nature reveals wisdom through colors, through the vibrancy of fruits, vegetables, and botanicals. The world around us thrives in rich hues, and so too should we. By consuming foods that carry the brilliance of Earth – deep greens, radiant reds, golden yellows – we, too, absorb this radiant aliveness, which reflects in our skin, our energy, our very essence.

We are what we ingest, in form and in frequency. Eat consciously, and become a vessel for clarity, for vitality, for the divine harmony that weaves through all living things.

To eat purely is to think purely. To nourish with integrity is to live with clarity. This is the path of refinement, of elevation, of honoring the sacred vessel that carries the soul.

Key Takeaways from Lesson I

The mind is a river that must be guided with intention to cultivate clarity and wisdom.

The brain breathes – this respiratory function plays a key role in perception and consciousness.

Stillness is the gateway to presence, allowing wisdom to surface unobstructed.

Neuroplasticity confirms that focused awareness reshapes the mind's structure, supporting discipline and resilience.

Health reflects mental clarity; as we discipline the mind, the body follows in vitality and the spirit in harmony.

Elevating our words and intellect refines the way we interact with the world.

Consciousness is an unfolding journey, progressing through levels of awakening.

Inner peace is found not by conquering the external world but by ending the battle within.

The organs, like the mind, must be treated with reverence for overall well-being.

A pure diet sharpens mental clarity, aligning us with higher frequencies.

Reflect & Apply Worksheet

1. Describe a recent situation where your thoughts were undisciplined. How did this impact your emotions and actions?

2. What is one habitual thought pattern you recognize as a distraction? How can you redirect this pattern toward clarity?

3. How does your breathing change throughout the day? What moments trigger shallow breathing, and how can you practice conscious breathwork?

4. Reflect on the connection between diet and clarity. What foods elevate your mental sharpness? What foods cause stagnation?

5. How can you incorporate stillness into your daily practice? What methods resonate most with you?

6. Identify where you are in the five levels of consciousness. What steps can you take to move toward the Luminous Sage?

To master the mind is to master one's path. This is the first step in aligning with *The Way that Knows*.

Lesson II: Training Your Breath

"Master the breath, let the self be in bliss, contemplate on the sublime within you." – Rig Veda

Breath is a bridge between seen and unseen, the thread that binds spirit to body, the silent architect of life's rhythm. Inhalation draws in sustenance; exhalation releases what no longer serves us. With every breath, we participate in the sacred cycle of renewal – an eternal dance between nourishment and release.

More than subtle oxygen, the air we breathe is imbued with life-giving forces: nitrogen for protein synthesis, oxygen for cellular energy, argon, carbon dioxide, and countless airborne bio-components – terpenes from the forest, negatively charged ions from waterfalls, subtle electromagnetic signals from Earth. Each inhalation is a communion with nature, an infusion of intelligence from winds that have circled the globe since time immemorial.

Pranayama, the ancient science of breath control, teaches that breath is more than sustenance, and is a force, a conduit for directing our will. The winds within us move in synergy with the winds of nature, and to train the breath is to cultivate harmony between inner and outer existence. When we breathe unconsciously, we are adrift, carried by external forces; when we breathe with intention, we reclaim authorship over our being.

To train the breath is to discipline the mind. Let each inhale be an invocation of clarity, an affirmation of discipline, a reminder that we are drawing in the essence of focus, strength, and purification. Let each exhale carry away attachment, stagnation, stress – anything that obstructs the path. Breath becomes a teacher, whispering of impermanence, guiding us to surrender, inviting us to become weightless in the flow of the present moment.

Breathwork is an alchemy of presence. When we consciously inhale, we engage the body's meridian system, channeling energy into the Nadis, the rivers of prana that flow through us. Deep, diaphragmatic breathing activates the vagus nerve, shifting us into a state of calm awareness, while rapid breath ignites the fire of transformation.

The sages and seers understood breath as a tool for enlightenment. The yogis of India, the Taoist masters of China, the shamans of the Americas – all trained the breath to unlock higher states of consciousness. The power of breath has been known since the great unfolding of all that is. This is not something to be learned, but to be remembered.

Sacred Breath

"Feelings come and go like clouds in a windy sky. Conscious breathing is my anchor." – Thich Nhat Hanh

In deep meditation, we become the breathing. There is no inhaler or exhaler – only a rhythmic tide of existence, a subtle pulse of life. Breath is a messenger of presence. A bridge between body and spirit. A sacred current that assures us we are alive.

Yet, in today's world, breath has been reduced to a mechanical function, estranged from the origin stories. The education system dismisses breath as a reflex, stripping away spiritual significance. The connection to spirit is under siege, suppressed by a culture that prioritizes industry over introspection. As reverence for breath is forgotten, so too is ethereal honor for life.

The attack on breath is not subtle. This is being woven into the fabric of modern existence. The movement, *I can't breathe,* was followed by wildfire engulfing nearly every region of the world, then a pandemic targeting the lungs. Masks were mandated, fresh air restricted, and fear became a greater pollutant than any industrial toxin. Few questioned the synchronicity. Fewer still recognized the lesson: we have forgotten to honor the breath.

How often do we extend gratitude for the oxygen we inhale? How often do we acknowledge the plankton and trees, the forests and oceans that gift us our very life force? Breath is a relationship, a sacred exchange. The Earth offers; we receive. We exhale; Earth is nourished in return. This reciprocity is delicate, a balance that must be honored.

Just as air sustains us, so too does oxygen purify. With every breath, we shed what is stagnant, cleansing our inner landscape. In the ways we must purify the body, we must also protect the world that sustains us.

Our respiratory tract is lined with epithelial cells, a sacred barrier between self and environment. They stand as guardians, filtering impurities, in a way how forests filter the toxins of the world. If we pollute our bodies with chemicals, processed foods, and synthetic compounds, we weaken this defense. If we pollute the Earth, we choke the lungs of the world.

To breathe with awareness is to remember our place in the greater cycle. We are to inhale with gratitude and exhale with reverence. We recognize that every breath is a gift, a silent prayer, a whisper of divine moving through us. When we honor the breath, we honor life. When we train the breath, we train the mind, the body, the soul – to move with the rhythm of creation, to exist in harmony with the winds that have carried wisdom for eternity.

Oxygen Is the Life Force of Renewal

"A single breath of pure awareness is more powerful than a thousand unmindful inhalations." — Lama Yeshe

Breath is a sustainer of life, the silent nourishment we often take for granted. Respiratory inspiration purifies blood, energizes cells, and carries unseen wisdom from the cosmos. Just as the tides are ceaseless, so too is the exchange of air – an endless cycle of giving and receiving, linking us to the greater whole.

Lungs are sacred vessels, expanding and contracting with every breath, but they atrophy in proportion to the density of foods we consume. The more we focus on filling our bellies, the less space we provide our lungs to fully expand. This lesson reminds us that true sustenance is found in the quality of air we breathe. Deep breaths, forceful exhalations, fresh air, and movement are pillars of vitality.

The purest air is found where nature thrives. High altitudes rich in ozone, forests dense with ferns, and waterfalls abundant in negative ions offer the most nourishing breath. These biocomponents cleanse the epithelium lining our respiratory tract, reinforcing our immunity and sharpening our awareness.

Every exhalation is a release, transmuting impurities that have been converted to gases and expelling them from the body. To breathe mindfully in pristine air, under the warmth of the sun, is to engage in a sacred act of purification. In such a state, the entire bloodstream can be cleansed in a single day.

Our world is riddled with attacks on breath – pollution, industrial toxins, and stagnant air in enclosed spaces. What many refer to as *common colds* are often symptoms of carbonic acid buildup from breathing stale air. Our lungs, the chief organs of digestion, absorb not just oxygen but cosmic nitrogen, which acts as a tissue builder and vitalizer. Hydrogen soothes the nerves, and oxygen sustains cells.

We hold the power to revere this sacred breath or surrender to conditions that diminish us. A resilient body defends, while a depleted one submits. Modern conditioning has lulled us into passivity, accepting toxic air as fate. Yet even the smallest exposure accumulates, quietly siphoning our vitality. We are not separate from our environment – we are in constant communion.

To heal is to reclaim our breath, to return to nature, to fill our lungs with pure air and empty them with intention. The quickest way to purify the blood is to breathe deeply, forcefully, with reverence. The simplest cure has always been before us. Step outside. Breathe. Let air be thy medicine.

Activating the Sacred Blueprint

"Breath links the finite to the boundless, connecting life to consciousness, which unites your body to your thoughts." — Thích Nhất Hạnh

Professor Hilton Hotema taught that air chambers in the skull are sacred transmitters of spiritual consciousness. These hollows are not empty but alive with energy, acting as conduits between breath and spirit. The small glands in the skull – the pineal, pituitary, and hypothalamus – are intellectual and spiritual centers, activated by the breath of life. The skull, he insisted, is the seat of divine intelligence, where instinct is heightened through proper cultivation of breath.

The strength of our nerves in the nose and sinuses determines the depth of our connection with spirit. Hotema emphasized that physical food nourishes the body, but spiritual food is what we breathe. Breathing is mechanical, yet spirit is the force inhaled – the cosmic intelligence that orchestrates the body's involuntary functions. When we take in a breath, this sacred current enters through the nostrils, moves into the spiritual chambers, travels to the lungs, and is absorbed into the bloodstream, feeding every cell.

When air is polluted, these sacred receptors become dormant. The degeneration of the body, weakening of physical senses, and disconnect from spiritual powers all stem from this assault on breath.

The modern world bombards us with corrosive acids – benzenes, ferrous oxide, hydrocyanic acid, methane, nitric acid – compromising our vitality. These contaminants poison the blood, attack the respiratory tract, and interfere with the body's natural intelligence.

Hotema warned that carbon dioxide buildup in enclosed spaces dulls the brain and depletes the lungs. In winter, indoor air can contain dangerously high levels of CO_2. The solution is simple: get outside. Breathe. Cold air contains a higher percentage of oxygen than warm air, reminding us that even in the stillness of winter, nature provides what we need.

He also taught that the lungs are chief organs of digestion. Cosmic nitrogen received through the breath builds tissue, oxygen supports cellular life, and hydrogen moistens the lungs and soothes the nervous system. This sacred chemistry affirms that breath is more than mere survival but is also spiritual sustenance.

Our bodies are designed to detoxify, yet modern conditioning has made us passive, willing to adapt to conditions that degrade our vitality. The weak body tolerates pollution because there is a lack of energy required to resist. The conditioned mind believes in invincibility, failing to recognize the slow accumulation of toxicity, but a little goes a long way. Even minor exposure compounds over time, creating vibratory hindrances that dull the senses and weaken the will.

The air we breathe determines our clarity, our vitality, and our ability to receive higher wisdom. The sacred chambers within the skull exist to guide us, but only when they are activated through clean air, deep breathing, and spiritual intention. If we wish to commune with divine intelligence, we must first clear the pathways, allowing the breath of life to move through us unobstructed.

To breathe is to receive. To exhale is to release. Let each breath be a prayer, a remembrance, a return to the sacred intelligence that lives within.

Mindful Breathing Techniques

Breath is the first nourishment, the primal sustenance that animates us before we ever taste food or water. In an era where our ability to breathe freely is threatened, we reclaim sovereignty over our breath through mindful practice.

A teacher once told me, *"To release impurities, you must exhale with force."* Coyotes know this. When poisoned, they sprint, panting heavily to expel toxins. We, too, can purge what does not belong by moving, by running, by breathing with intention.

Breathwork Exercises for Clarity, Focus, and Resilience:

Box Breathing (Fourfold Breath): Inhale for four counts, hold for four counts, exhale for four counts, hold for four counts. This technique steadies the nervous system and sharpens focus.

The Purification Breath: Inhale deeply through the nose, feeling the breath cleanse from crown to root. Hold briefly, then exhale through the mouth, releasing all that is impure.

Alternate Nostril Breathing (Nadi Shodhana): Close one nostril, inhale deeply through the other, switch nostrils, and exhale. This balances the brain hemispheres and clears energetic blockages.

Breath of Fire: A rapid, rhythmic inhalation and exhalation through the nose, powered by the diaphragm. This ignites inner heat, burns away stagnation, and awakens the vital force within.

4-2-6-2 Rhythm: Inhale for four seconds, hold for two, exhale with force for six, and release further through the nose for two. This practice strengthens lung capacity and purifies the blood.

To breathe with awareness is to reclaim the self. Breath is presence, discipline, and renewal. Let your respiration guide you on *The Way that Knows.*

Key Takeaways from Lesson II

Breath is the bridge between the physical and the spiritual, linking body to mind and guiding us into alignment with the divine.

Breathwork is the first form of nourishment, sustaining life before food or water and influencing every function in the body.

Conscious breath is a tool for discipline, focus, and clarity which trains the mind, settles the body, and strengthens the spirit.

Ancient traditions understood breath as a key to enlightenment – yogis, Taoist sages, and shamans all used breathing techniques to elevate consciousness.

Modern life often restricts our ability to breathe freely – pollution, indoor living, stress, and poor posture compromise the full expansion of the lungs.

Different breathing techniques offer specific benefits, from calming the nervous system to increasing resilience, detoxification, and energy.

The lungs are sacred organs, responsible not just for respiration but for filtering toxins and purifying the blood.

Cold, oxygen-rich air invigorates the body and mind, while stagnant, polluted air contributes to illness and mental dullness.

Forceful exhalation is a powerful detoxifier, helping remove stagnation, impurities, and emotional blockages.

Reconnecting with breath in nature – by breathing deeply in forests, near waterfalls, and in fresh mountain air – restores clarity and well-being.

Reflect & Apply Worksheet

1. How often do you pay attention to your breath? What moments throughout your day do you find yourself holding your breath or breathing shallowly?

2. What emotions arise when you take slow, deep breaths? How does intentional breathing shift your state of mind?

3. Experiment with one of the mindful breathing techniques listed in this lesson. Which one resonates with you most, and how does it affect your mental clarity and physical energy?

4. How can you incorporate more fresh air into your life? What changes can you make to spend more time breathing deeply in nature?

5. Reflect on how breath influences movement. How does your breath feel when you exercise, when you are still, and when you are engaged in deep focus?

6. Observe your environment – does the air you breathe feel nourishing or stagnant? How can you improve the quality of the air you inhale daily?

7. In what ways can you train your breath to be a tool for discipline and purification? How can this practice support your journey on *The Way that Knows*?

Breath is the rhythm of existence, the ever-present guide that moves through us, sustaining and purifying. By training our breath, we train our mind. By honoring our breath, we honor life. Let this practice be a return to wholeness, a reclamation of presence, and a path toward greater clarity and wisdom.

Lesson III: Restoring Fluidity in the Body

"Water is fluid, soft, and yielding. But water will wear away rock, which is rigid and cannot yield. This is another paradox: What is soft is strong." — Lao Tzu

Divinity flows through fluid. The rivers on Earth carry currents of life, shaping landscapes, nourishing forests, and sustaining ecosystems. When water moves freely, the world thrives, but when a dam is placed upon a river, when stagnation sets in, life downstream suffers. This same principle applies to the body. Movement of our fluids – unobstructed circulation of blood, lymph, cerebrospinal fluid, and interstitial fluid – is the foundation of primordial energy. Where flow exists, health follows. Where stagnation arises, disease begins.

Breath, the great mover of life, is the key to fluidity. Each inhale directs the tides within, and each exhale releases what no longer serves. Through breath, we animate circulation; we awaken the divine orders of nature within our internal waters. When our breath is deep and rhythmic, blood cleanses, the lymphatic system drains impurities, and cerebrospinal fluid bathes the brain in renewal. Yet, when the breath is shallow, when the body remains still, stagnation accumulates like a dammed river, obstructing divine flow.

Movement is the sacred act of keeping our internal rivers flowing. Lack of movement, coupled with a reliance on processed, dense foods, burdens our circulation. Plaque in our arteries slows the river of life. Congested bowels prevent the excretion of waste. High-fat diets, especially those saturated with cooked oils and fats – whether from plants or animals – thicken blood and hinder the ability to nourish cells. The debate of omnivore versus vegan is secondary to the greater principle: pure blood sustains the body, and stagnation invites decay.

Learning From Nature's Divine Fluidity

"Stagnation is the root of disease. Motion, the secret of life." –
Avicenna

The body is an intricate system of flowing currents. The heart pumps blood, lymphatic system drains toxins, and cerebrospinal fluid nourishes the nervous system. These systems do not function in isolation; they are unified by breath. Shallow breathing allows stagnation to accumulate, while deep, intentional breath fuels circulation, keeps energy moving, and prevents obstructions from forming.

If we are not moving our bodies, what we eat becomes secondary to the fact that we are depriving our internal systems of the motion they require. Sedentary living causes disorders, even for those who are purists in their diet. The breath, the pulse of our life force, must be accompanied by action.

Move your body, often, and with intention. Let movement be your medicine. Step outside and breathe air that has danced with the trees. Ride a bike through the hills, feeling your lungs expand with each ascent. Skip if you must. Dance to the rhythm of the wind. Exert your body to the point of deep inhalation, allowing your breath to reach the depths of your being. To breathe is to move; to move is to flow.

A teacher once told me, *"If you wish to purify your blood, you must exhale with force."* The coyote knows this truth. When poisoned by a trapper, she does not succumb – she runs. She sprints with ferocity, forcing her breath to move through her body, expelling the toxins that would otherwise claim her life. She does not wait for stagnation to take hold; she moves, she breathes, she purifies.

We, too, must learn this wisdom. The breath is our purifier, our cleanser, our healer. If the body is burdened with waste, the breath will attempt to expel through coughing, sneezing, and perspiration. To ignore this process, and to suppress with medications or sedentary habits, is to obstruct the natural order.

The Body's Sacred Waters

"Just as a lotus rises untainted from the murky waters, so too must one purify the inner waters of the body, for they reflect the clarity of the mind and the lightness of the spirit." – Siddhartha Gautama

The human body is a vast internal ocean, composed of multiple essential fluids that sustain life and facilitate optimal function. When these waters flow without obstruction, health is maintained; when they stagnate, illness emerges.

Blood – Delivers oxygen and nutrients to every cell while removing metabolic waste. Healthy blood flow is necessary for immune function, tissue regeneration, and overall vitality.

Lymph – A clear fluid that drains toxins, metabolic waste, and cellular debris from tissues, circulating immune cells to protect against disease.

Cerebrospinal Fluid – Bathes the brain and spinal cord, carrying nutrients while removing toxins, critical for neurological clarity and cognitive function.

Interstitial Fluid – Surrounds and nourishes cells, facilitating communication between tissues and enabling the transport of oxygen and nutrients.

Synovial Fluid – Lubricates joints, reducing friction and ensuring smooth movement.

Saliva – Begins the digestion process, neutralizes harmful bacteria, and supports oral and gut health.

Gastric Juices – Aid in breaking down food and absorbing nutrients, essential for metabolism and digestion.

Bile – Produced by the liver, bile emulsifies fats and facilitates detoxification.

Pancreatic Fluid – Neutralizes stomach acid and supports digestion of proteins, fats, and carbohydrates.

Urine – Eliminates metabolic waste and toxins from the blood, maintaining electrolyte balance.

Sweat – Cools the body while expelling toxins and maintaining mineral balance.

Tears – Protect and lubricate the eyes, removing debris and reducing inflammation.

Mucus – Lines the respiratory and digestive tracts, trapping pathogens and facilitating immune defense.

Breast Milk – Provides essential nutrients, immune protection, and growth factors to infants.

Pericardial Fluid – Cushions the heart and reduces friction between its layers.

Pleural Fluid – Prevents friction between the lungs and chest wall, aiding respiration.

Endolymph and Perilymph – Maintain equilibrium in the inner ear, ensuring balance and spatial awareness.

Each of these sacred waters plays a vital role in maintaining homeostasis. When stagnation occurs, purification is necessary. The key to sustaining the flow of these life-giving fluids lies in movement, hydration, and breathwork.

Cessation of Stagnation

"A healthy body is like a flowing river; the energy moves through, cleansing and renewing every cell. When stagnation occurs, disease takes hold." — Paramahansa Yogananda

Stagnation is the root of all dysfunctions, the slow erosion of vitality as stillness settles into places where movement once thrived. The body is designed for perpetual flow, an intricate system of currents and tides, yet modern habits have turned most human terrains into reservoirs where stagnation festers.

When fluids cease to move, they begin to degrade – blood thickens, lymph stagnates, interstitial spaces become congested, and cellular communication is impaired. This is how illness begins, not as an abrupt event but as the cumulative effect of blocked pathways and interrupted flow.

Water in the natural world tells us everything we need to know about health. A mountain stream, clear and rushing, carries minerals, oxygen, and etheric charge. Compare this to a stagnant pond, where algae bloom unchecked, oxygen is depleted, and decomposition takes hold. Our internal waters follow the same laws. When fluids move freely, we regenerate. When they stagnate, waste accumulates, and life force diminishes.

Movement is the great liberator, breath the great purifier. Every cell in the body requires hydration and circulation to function optimally. If we are sedentary, we become like the still pond, our inner terrain choked by stagnation. But when we move with intention – through breath, through exercise, through mindful engagement with our environment – we reclaim our natural rhythm. The cessation of stagnation is a return to fluidity, the reminder that life is motion, and where there is movement, there is renewal.

Purification and Nourishment of the Body's Fluids

"Water is the elixir of life, giver of strength, purifier of sins. As flows within, so cleanses the spirit, bringing harmony to the self." – Rig Veda

Every drop of water within us carries memory of ancient rivers, celestial rains, and the pulsations of the universe. The fluids of our body are not simply biological components; they are vessels of conductivity, carriers of intelligence, and conduits of energy that sustain our vitality. To purify and nourish these fluids is to refine the internal channels through which life force flows, aligning the physical with the divine.

In this practice of purification, hydration is just the beginning. Movement stirs the internal tides, breathwork oxygenates the currents, and nourishment replenishes the sacred reservoirs within. Sound and frequency can restore vibrational integrity, reattuning our inner waters to their original harmony. The body, much like the Earth, thrives when our rivers run pure, tides are balanced, and essence remains unpolluted.

Hydration: Proper hydration ensures that all bodily fluids remain in motion. Spring water, structured water, and electrolytes are essential for maintaining cellular hydration and conductivity.

Movement: Regular exercise stimulates circulation, lymphatic drainage, and detoxification. Activities like rebounding, stretching, and dynamic movement facilitate fluid flow.

Breathwork: Deep diaphragmatic breathing moves lymph, enhances cerebrospinal circulation, and oxygenates blood.

Dietary Support: Consuming water-rich fruits, raw vegetables, and herbal infusions nourishes and replenishes bodily fluids. Avoiding dehydrating substances like processed foods, caffeine, and alcohol prevents stagnation.

Sound Therapy and Biohacking Treatments: Frequencies from sound therapy, PEMF therapy, infrared saunas, and hydrotherapy can help restore vibrational coherence in bodily fluids, promoting optimal function.

Restoring Flow

"Water is the first principle of all things, and within the human body, is the living vessel of light, carrying the memory of health or disease. Keep pure, you will be kept whole." – Paracelsus

To restore fluidity, we must honor the sacred relationship between breath and movement.

Breath-Infused Motion – Engage in daily movement that synchronizes with deep breathing. Whether through yoga, Qi Gong, or simple stretching, let the breath lead the body, guiding circulation and preventing stagnation.

Lymphatic Activation – The lymphatic system, unlike the circulatory system, has no pump. This system relies on muscle contractions and deep breathing. Rebounding, dry brushing, and deep belly breathing stimulate lymphatic drainage and detoxification.

Cerebrospinal Fluid Renewal – Inversions, spinal waves, and craniosacral work help move cerebrospinal fluid, nourishing the brain and nervous system. Conscious breathwork can amplify this effect, allowing for heightened clarity and spiritual receptivity.

Exhalation Purification – Forceful exhalations help release stagnation from the blood and lungs. Sprinting, high-intensity movement, and deep sighs aid in the removal of toxins.

Hydration and Flow – Water, the medium of life, must move within us just as through rivers. Proper hydration, combined with movement and breath, ensures that all fluids remain in motion.

The Way That Knows moves like water – effortless, fluid, without obstruction. To align with this way, we must become fluid ourselves. We must dissolve rigidity in both body and mind, ensuring that nothing dams the rivers of our internal world.

Breathe deeply. Move often. Let your fluids flow freely, and in doing so, allow divinity to move through you unobstructed.

Key Takeaways from Lesson III

The movement of bodily fluids is the key to vitality. Where fluids flow, health thrives; where stagnation arises, disease takes hold.

Breath is the primary mover of internal circulation – oxygenating blood, stimulating lymphatic drainage, and supporting cerebrospinal fluid flow.

Just as rivers nourish the land, bodily fluids must move unobstructed to maintain cellular renewal and detoxification.

Lack of movement, processed foods, and environmental toxins create stagnation, leading to chronic disease.

The body contains seventeen sacred fluids, each essential for function, purification, and homeostasis.

Water in nature teaches us the importance of flow – stagnant water breeds disease, while moving water nourishes life.

Movement, hydration, breathwork, and intentional purification practices ensure optimal fluid circulation.

Stagnation is the silent thief of vitality, and the only cure is to move, breathe, and restore flow.

Reflect & Apply Worksheet

1. **Observe Your Flow:** Take a moment to assess your body. Where do you feel stagnant? Where do you feel fluid? Identify any areas that feel heavy, inflamed, or constricted.

2. **Breath Awareness:** Throughout your day, notice how deeply you breathe. Are you breathing fully and expansively, or is your breath shallow? How does your breath change with movement?

3. **Hydration Check:** Reflect on your daily water intake. Are you drinking enough structured, mineral-rich water to support your body's fluidity? How can you improve your hydration practices?

4. **Movement Assessment:** Consider how often you move. Do you sit for long periods without stretching? How can you incorporate more breath-infused movement into your daily routine?

5. **Lymphatic Activation:** Try rebounding, dry brushing, or deep belly breathing for a few minutes each day. Notice any changes in energy levels, clarity, or digestion.

6. **Nature Connection:** Reflect on how often you immerse yourself in nature's fluidity. When was the last time you swam in a river, walked barefoot in the dew, or stood beneath a waterfall? How does this affect your internal flow?

7. **Personal Commitment:** What is one daily action you will take to restore and maintain fluidity in your body? Write this down and commit for the next week.

Lesson IV: Microbiome Rebalancing

The body is a diverse ecosystem, home to trillions of microorganisms that govern our radiance, clarity, and overall well-being. Our microbiome – the vast network of bacteria, fungi, and other microbes that inhabit our body – is not just an accessory to health; but is an organ, influencing every system, from digestion to cognition to immune resilience. When harmony exists within this microbial world, we thrive. When imbalance takes hold, stagnation, inflammation, and disease emerge.

The Microbiome as a Living Organ

The microbiome is an invisible yet omnipresent force, a self-regulating intelligence within us that adapts to our lifestyle, diet, and environment. Like all organs, this is alive, has rhythm, function, and frequency. Scientists have begun to recognize what ancient wisdom has long understood: our microbiome is a vital aspect of our overall health, influencing not only digestion but also mental clarity, emotional resilience, and immune strength. When dysbiosis – an imbalance in gut bacteria – takes hold, our inner world begins to break down, leading to brain fog, inflammation, mood disturbances, and metabolic dysfunction.

Our environment shapes our microbiome. Just as animals in a forest have a sacredly distinct microbial terrain than those in captivity, humans who dwell in cities possess a vastly different microbial landscape than those living in the wilderness. Studies have shown that indigenous people, untouched by industrialized foods and pollution, maintain diverse and robust microbiomes.

In contrast, modern lifestyles – filled with processed foods, chemical-laden water, hand sanitizers, and pharmaceutical interventions – have led to a mass extinction event within our gut microbiota. The microbiome of ancient humans was rich with species now absent in industrialized societies. With this loss of microbial diversity, we have seen a rise in digestive disorders, autoimmune diseases, and even mental health conditions linked to gut-brain dysregulation.

Gut Instinct – Can We Really Trust Our Gut?

What comes first – our consciousness or the microorganisms that develop symbiotic relationships with our cells, organs, and nerves? If the body were void of microbes, would we still have the same capacity to think, perceive, and communicate? Could our intelligence, health, and even the thoughts that circulate our mind be ephemeral reflections of the collective microbial consciousness inhabiting us? The trillions of microbes residing within us form an intricate web of intelligence, operating as a biome within a biome – a self-regulating ecosystem influencing not only digestion but also emotions, instincts, and decision-making.

The cliché adage tells us to *trust our gut*, but have we ever questioned what, or *who*, is truly guiding that instinct? The gut, after all, is not just an organ. Our gut is an entire landscape teeming with microbial life. These microorganisms influence our appetite, cravings, and even our moods. If gut flora is imbalanced, and overridden by pathogenic or virulent microbes, can we truly trust the signals being transmitted to our brain? When we hesitate to make a necessary change, when we resist stepping into a higher state of being, is that hesitation truly ours – or is this an indication of microbial consciousness resisting an environment that no longer supports the survival of something foreign in the terrain?

Consider the moment an infant is born. Are they entering the world with an independent, fully human consciousness, or are they developing a consciousness shaped by microbial populations colonizing their inner landscape? When we nourish ourselves with foods that promote vitality, our gut flora aligns with the intelligence of nature. If we feed ourselves lifeless, processed, and chemical-laden substances, we cultivate an internal ecosystem that operates at a lower vibrational frequency. When our gut directs us toward destructive habits, this is not a whisper of wisdom. What we are experiencing is the desperate plea of an imbalanced microbiome seeking to maintain dominion within our expanse. This is a signal from a distorted frequency in the body.

Microbes communicate with us through our nerves, influencing desires, habits, and even the people and environments we gravitate toward. This symbiotic relationship mirrors the way mycelium networks, and mycorrhizal connections allow forests to communicate underground, carrying signals between trees, fungi, and plant roots. Just as nature thrives when mycelial networks remain intact, we thrive when our gut microbiome is in balance. This internal equilibrium refines our instincts, sharpens our discernment, and ensures that what we feel compelled to do is truly in alignment with our highest good.

A microbiome in balance emits a frequency that harmonizes with the rhythms of nature. When our inner ecosystem is thriving, we are naturally drawn toward higher-frequency people, environments, and experiences. The microbes within us radiate energy, influencing our electromagnetic field and determining what we attract. The more we align with nature, the more we shed cravings that do not serve us. A healthy gut, enriched by diverse plant foods, naturally disciplines us to seek only what nourishes and uplifts. If our gut is leading us toward toxicity – whether in the form of artificial foods, pharmaceutical drugs, or destructive lifestyle patterns – then we are not following instinct, but rather the cries of an imbalanced terrain. We are likely being influenced by rogue particles of decay and corrupting whispers in the flesh.

Everything we ingest – whether food, air, water, or the subtle energies of our surroundings – intertwines with our consciousness. This understanding compels me to lean deeper into nature's wisdom. I chew on the resin clinging to trees, absorbing medicinal intelligence. I rest my forehead against ponderosa pine bark and let the moss cradle my senses. I dig my hands into redwood soil, press my bare feet into mud, and breathe in the rich scent of ferns swaying in the wind. I avoid artificial landscapes and seek wild places, untamed forests, and open sky. I eat freshly picked fruits, imbibe the purity of living water, and allow nature's abundance to recalibrate my being. Through this, I know my instincts are not corrupted by interference – I am guided by the language of life.

Gut-Brain Connection and Mental Clarity

The gut is often referred to as the *second brain*, and for good reason. The microbiota residing in our digestive system directly influences neurotransmitter production, immune response, and even emotional well-being. A dysregulated gut can lead to increased anxiety, depression, and cognitive fog, while a thriving microbiome fosters mental sharpness, emotional stability, and resilience. Studies show that individuals with a balanced gut microbiome demonstrate lower cortisol levels and greater capacity for focus and clarity.

Many who seek enlightenment or spiritual clarity fail to recognize that their mental and emotional state is deeply intertwined with the microbial terrain of their gut. Celestial clarification of the mind is impossible without purification of the gut. If we seek wisdom and heightened awareness, we must first rebalance the microbiome, ensuring that the bacteria we cultivate support clarity rather than chaos.

Intelligence of the Microbiome

Our microbiome is an ecosystem, much like a forest or coral reef, teeming with life that thrives in balance. When we consume whole, natural foods and interact with the natural world – walking barefoot, breathing in the air of forests, touching the soil – our microbial communities diversify and strengthen. In contrast, urban environments, sterile living conditions, and processed foods disrupt this balance, leading to dysbiosis and chronic disease.

This understanding challenges the common phrase, *trust your gut.* Can we truly trust our instinct when our gut is overrun by microbes that thrive on processed foods, pharmaceuticals, and synthetic chemicals? Are our cravings truly our own, or are they signals sent by an imbalanced microbiome demanding sustenance for survival? Are we allowing our intestines to house low-vibrational intruders, phantoms of sickness and toxic invaders?

Many times, hesitation and fear come not from intuition but from the microbial intelligence residing within us. When we experience resistance to detoxification or lifestyle changes, this is often because the pathogenic microbes that have colonized our system perceive a threat to their survival.

The best way to make clear decisions, especially regarding significant life changes, is to first cleanse the body. By rebalancing the microbiome, we restore microbial consciousness to a state that supports clarity, intuition, and optimal well-being. A gut inhabited by high-vibrational microbial communities supports clarity of thought and the ability to discern what is truly in alignment with our higher self.

Microbes emit subtle electromagnetic frequencies, influencing our energetic field and shaping the connections we make. A balanced microbiome resonates at a frequency that attracts relationships, experiences, and environments that serve our highest good. In contrast, toxic gut terrain may magnetize experiences that reflect stagnation, confusion, or self-destructive patterns.

Rewilding and Reconnecting with Nature's Intelligence

The best way to restore microbial health is to rewild – returning to nature to replenish what has been lost. Walk barefoot, let your skin touch the Earth, breathe in the biome of the forests, and immerse yourself in wild waters. Eat freshly picked fruits, inhale the aroma of raw tree sap, and let the scent of moss and ferns enter your lungs. These interactions rebuild microbial diversity, awakening dormant pathways of intuition and vitality.

When we step into nature, we expand our consciousness. The intelligence of our microbiome mirrors the intelligence of the Earth. To restore balance within is to restore balance with the greater whole. By caring for our internal terrain, we not only reclaim health – we realign with *The Way That Knows*.

Plant-Based Potency

The intelligence of nature is encoded in plants – pure, uncorrupted, and imbued with the elemental forces of the Earth and cosmos. When we consume plants, we absorb not only their nutrients but also the vibrational imprints of sunlight, soil minerals, and electromagnetic energies of the natural world. This is why I remain devoted to a plant-based life: not as a diet, but as a communion with wisdom stored in the plant queendom.

I no longer eat solely to appease hunger. I eat to inherit consciousness within the foods I consume. When we reach a certain level of internal cleanliness, our body no longer craves food as a coping mechanism or a means of filling voids. Hunger evolves. We begin to see food as a teacher, an energy that informs our cells, our mind, and our spirit. To eat consciously is to seek nourishment beyond sustenance. We consume with the intent of refinement, expansion, and vitality.

If something is dead, and has already begun the process of decay, this belongs in the soil, returning to the cycle of decomposition. My body is not a graveyard for what has been slaughtered. Life cannot be cultivated from consuming death. This principle extends beyond animal products – this includes processed foods, chemically treated crops, and even cooked plant-based foods that have lost their vibrational charge. Heat reduces voltage, strips vital energy, and diminishes the radiance of what we ingest. When I eat, I attune to the life force of my food, ensuring that what I ingest invigorates rather than dulls my consciousness.

The synergy of fresh air, mindful breathwork, movement, and clean nutrition activates the cosmic intelligence within and around us. Every inhalation, every barefoot step on the Earth, every bite of food grown under the sun aligns us more deeply with nature's rhythm. This is why my plant-based philosophy extends beyond mere abstinence from animal products. I avoid cooked oils, gluten, heated salts, synthetic yeast, soy, alcohol, pharmaceuticals, and all that is artificial. These substances do not serve my body's frequency, nor do they contribute to my elevation.

There was a time when different dietary approaches served me, particularly in my youth as a competitive athlete. But through years of refinement, I have found that this way of eating allows me to radiate light, to sharpen my cognitive faculties, and to sustain the highest vibratory state possible. Each vibrant meal I consume is a gift – a direct infusion of nature's intelligence, an offering of clarity, strength, and illumination.

We are what we ingest, in form and in frequency. Eat consciously, and become a vessel for clarity, for vitality, for the divine harmony that weaves through all living things.

Eat Colorful Foods

Of the estimated 400,000 plants dancing on Earth today, only around four percent – roughly 16,000 – are known to be edible. Of these, humans regularly consume a mere 150-200, with seventy-five percent of the world's food supply generated from just twelve plants and five animal species. Imagine how much more vibrant and nourishing our diets could be if we embraced the full spectrum of plant life, rather than limiting ourselves to a narrow, industrialized selection. Imagine a world where the energy funneled into destruction was instead redirected toward making these life-giving foods accessible to all.

Nature's palette is rich with colors that carry distinct bioenergetic frequencies, yet modern industrialized foods have displaced these natural pigments with synthetic coloring agents. The vital force within food has been stripped, and the innate intelligence replaced with chemical imitations that deceive the senses while starving the cells. Why remove the life-giving pigments that activate our antioxidant defense system? Why replace nature's innate medicine with artificial substitutes that deplete rather than restore?

True nourishment comes from a diet rich in phytonutrient biodiversity – compounds found in the vibrant colors of fruits, vegetables, roots, and herbs. These pigments serve as messengers of vitality, influencing our gut microbiome, immune function, and cognitive clarity. There are approximately 25,000 phytonutrients in natural foods, yet most items found in modern grocery stores contain none. Instead, they are laden with advanced glycation end products (AGEs), synthetic preservatives, and microbial disruptors that fuel inflammation and stagnation within the body.

A city, or any unhealthy environment disconnected from nature, can be labeled a *dysbiosphere*. Many grocery stores fall into this same category – offering shelves lined with lifeless, processed products that do nothing to sustain health. I have walked through vast supermarkets without finding a single item worthy of consumption. How could an entire store be devoted to food, yet only one small section in a single aisle is labeled as "natural" or "healthy"? What does this imply about everything else being sold? The answer is clear: true nourishment is not found in industrialized food systems, but in the untouched abundance of the Earth.

A great way to break free from this manufactured cycle is to stop relying on conventional retail grocers and instead support farmers' markets, permaculture farms, and community-owned food collectives. Eating in harmony with nature means embracing seasonal diversity, foraging where possible, and choosing foods that are alive, intact, and infused with the energies of the sun, soil, and sky.

When we choose food in the most natural state, we choose to align with life. The more colorful our plates, the more vibrant our cells. The more diverse our nourishment, the more balanced our microbiome. Every bite is an opportunity – to heal, to regenerate, and to move closer to a state of higher consciousness.

Factors That Disrupt Microbial Balance

Several elements contribute to microbial imbalances, leading to dysbiosis and health deterioration:

Antibiotics and Medications – While sometimes necessary, antibiotics wipe out beneficial bacteria, creating an imbalance that may take years to repair. Pharmaceutical drugs alter microbial terrain, often causing long-term damage.

Industrialized Diets – Processed foods, sugars, and artificial additives feed pathogenic bacteria, while depleting beneficial microbes. Yogurt, often marketed as a probiotic-rich health food, contains carcinogenic compounds and synthetic additives that disrupt gut balance rather than restore.

Environmental Toxins – Pesticides, glyphosate, heavy metals, and pollutants poison our microbiome, leading to chronic inflammation and weakened immunity.

Sanitized Lifestyles – Our ancestors were exposed to rich microbial environments through soil, plants, and fresh air. Today, over-sanitization and disconnection from nature have led to weakened microbial diversity.

Emotional Stress and Hormonal Imbalance – The microbes within us feed on the chemicals we produce. Chronic stress, anxiety, and fear nourish pathogenic bacteria, leading to cycles of emotional instability and dependency on harmful mental states.

Purification and Rebalancing Strategies

Restoring microbial balance requires a return to nature, nourishment, and intentional detoxification.

Kambo and Peptide Therapy – The secretion from the Kambo frog contains bioactive peptides that expel harmful microbes, yeast, fungi, and parasites. This ancient cleansing ritual is known to purge toxins, restore gut balance, and fortify the immune system.

Nourish with Prebiotics and Resistant Starch – Beneficial bacteria thrive on fibrous foods such as raw vegetables, green bananas, and tubers. These compounds encourage the proliferation of healthy microbes.

Rewild the Microbiome – Spending time in nature, interacting with soil, and immersing in forests introduces diverse bacteria that strengthen immunity and digestive health. Walking barefoot on the earth, gardening, and swimming in natural bodies of water replenish our microbial terrain.

Fasting and Gut Reset Protocols – Periodic fasting allows the digestive system to rest and supports microbial turnover. Extended fasting or juice cleansing helps eliminate overgrowth of harmful bacteria.

Colon Hydrotherapy and Coffee Enemas – These cleansing methods help remove mucoid plaque, rebalance microbial populations, and detoxify the liver, enabling the gut to function optimally.

Eliminate Processed and Inflammatory Foods – Remove refined sugars, industrial seed oils, processed grains, and chemical-laden products that degrade the microbiome.

Consume Living, Raw, and Fermented Foods Wisely – While some fermented foods can support gut health, caution should be taken with commercial yogurts and dairy-based probiotics, which can introduce harmful compounds rather than restore balance. Elect for plant-based ferments like raw sauerkraut, kimchi, and coconut kefir.

Emotional Detox and Breathwork – Releasing emotional trauma through conscious breathwork and meditation resets the gut-brain axis, preventing negative emotional states from feeding harmful bacteria.

The Microbiome as a Spiritual Gateway

If everything eventually becomes food for microbes, then what we cultivate within determines the energy we embody. A disordered microbiome clouds the mind, disrupts emotions, and weakens the spirit. When we restore balance, we align with clarity, peace, and intuition.

Microbes possess their own intelligence, influencing not only our cravings but our thoughts and desires. If we are governed by pathogenic bacteria, we will be drawn to processed foods, alcohol, and harmful substances. If we cultivate a thriving, high-frequency microbiome, we will crave life-giving nourishment, both physically and spiritually.

Modern research has confirmed what ancient wisdom has always known: microbial balance is the foundation of health. To purify the gut is to purify the mind. To harmonize the microbiome is to harmonize the self. The path of *The Way Knows* requires the restoration of inner ecology, ensuring that the body's internal world is as balanced and fluid as the universe.

A thriving microbiome is a thriving mind. A stagnant gut is a stagnant spirit. Choose the way of movement, of renewal, of clarity – and let your inner world reflect the divine order of nature.

Key Takeaways from Lesson IV

The microbiome is an intelligent, self-regulating ecosystem that directly influences digestion, immunity, and mental clarity.

A healthy gut microbiome contributes to emotional resilience, cognitive function, and even spiritual alignment.

Environmental factors such as pollution, over-sanitization, pesticides, and industrialized foods have led to a mass extinction of beneficial gut bacteria.

Studies confirm that ancient humans had a much richer microbial diversity compared to modern industrialized societies.

The microbiome interacts with consciousness, meaning our mental state, habits, and dietary choices influence the intelligence of our internal microbial world.

Dysbiosis – an imbalance in gut bacteria – leads to inflammation, digestive disorders, mental fog, and metabolic dysfunction.

Modern diets have replaced nutrient-dense, diverse foods with synthetic, chemical-laden substitutes that fuel microbial imbalance.

The best way to restore gut health is through rewilding – returning to natural foods, interacting with soil, fresh air, and consuming plant-based nourishment.

The microbiome emits subtle electromagnetic frequencies, affecting our energy field, thoughts, cravings, and even the types of relationships we attract.

Purification of the gut is necessary for heightened awareness and intuitive clarity – without a balanced microbiome, we cannot fully access higher states of consciousness.

Reflect & Apply Worksheet

1. **Assess Your Gut Health:** Reflect on your digestive patterns, mental clarity, and energy levels. Do you experience bloating, sluggishness, or brain fog? How might your gut microbiome be influencing your daily experience?

2. **Observe Your Cravings:** When you feel drawn to certain foods, pause and reflect – are these true bodily needs, or are they microbial signals from an imbalanced gut terrain? How can you shift your diet toward more nourishing, life-giving foods?

3. **Environmental Awareness:** Consider the environments you spend most of your time in. Are they rich in microbial diversity (forests, fresh air, soil) or stagnant (indoor, urban, sterile settings)? How can you expose yourself to more natural, life-enhancing surroundings?

4. **Microbiome Rebalancing Practices:** Which strategies from this lesson – fasting, consuming prebiotic-rich foods, incorporating Kambo or peptide therapy, rewilding – resonate most with you? What steps can you take to restore microbial balance?

5. **Mental & Emotional Connection:** Reflect on how your gut health affects your thoughts and emotions. Have you noticed patterns of fear, stress, or anxiety coinciding with poor digestion? How might purifying your microbiome support a clearer mind and more stable emotions?

6. **Color & Diversity in Food:** Observe your plate – do the contents contain vibrant, phytonutrient-rich foods, or are they lacking in color and diversity? How can you introduce more natural pigments and plant-based vitality into your meals?

7. **Personal Commitment:** What one practice will you implement today to support your microbiome health? Write this down and commit to this task for the next week.

The 2nd Realm: Aligning with Divine Orchestration

Lesson V: Strengthening Source Connection

There is a river beneath all things, a quantum stream of intelligence, guiding the breath of the wind, the flowering of the stars, the pulse within our chest. The ancients knew this river well, though she bore different names – the Hunab Ku of the Maya, the Inka's Kawsay Pacha, the Tao, the Prana, and the Great Spirit. They did not seek to conquer the river, nor did they attempt to exploit the energetic currents or corrupt the flow. They lived within this force, offered reverence, prayed intently, and listened.

To strengthen our connection to Source is not to create something new. This is more about remembering. To uncover what has always been. The divine is not distant, nor separate, but humming within each cell, woven into the light that feeds the leaves and the breath that animates our being.

Mayan priests whispered their prayers to the ceiba tree. Andean mystics opened their hearts upon the mountain peaks. Lakota seers sang their visions to the sky. Each knew that the bridge to the sacred is not built by words alone, but by the clarity of presence, by the purity of devotion. To pray is not to beg; but to align, to make oneself an instrument of divine harmony.

A clear prayer is not muddled with doubt. Affirmation does not plead from scarcity, nor seek to barter with the cosmos. A true prayer is a frequency, a resonance, an act of communion. Invocation is spoken with the knowing that what is asked has already been answered. This is the potency of *I AM*. When we say, *"I am love. I am peace. I am light,"* we are not summoning something outside ourselves, but activating an embodiment of innate morals, principles, and values that have never left us.

There is a reason the sages and mystics across time have turned to sound – the chanting of the Vedas, the Gregorian hymns, the sacred Ohm. This vibration, the cosmic syllable, is the voice of creation. When we intone Ohm, we attune ourselves to the divine heartbeat, merging the body with the great resonance of existence.

We are sustained by forces beyond the visible, drawing strength from more than mere sustenance. Supernal wisdom upholds our steps, guiding us with unseen currents. The journey enriches us with higher knowing, while the essence of the cosmos infuses us with vitality. Cosmic awareness nourishes the soul, and we partake in the endless flow of revelation. Each moment unveils a banquet of understanding. The sun streams forth silent energies, the breath channels life's essence, and the universe showers us with luminous whispers. Hilton Hotema wrote about absorbing light as life force, of the body's ability to drink in divine energy. This is the art of swallowing divinity – not in the literal sense, but in the way of absorption, of allowing the sacred to permeate all our being.

Spirit is not elsewhere. This numen is not hidden in distant realms or locked away in books. The life force of creation is the pulse of the earth beneath bare feet, the hush between waves, the light within our marrow. The Soulfire is within and is all around.

To connect with Source is to return home – not to a place, but to a knowing. To walk not in search of the divine, but in recognition that we have never been apart.

God Is All Around

I have learned over the years that God is far vaster and more interesting than religious narratives exclaim. The universal frequency that governs all life is more expansive than what one man could embody, more fluid than any single doctrine could contain. When my understanding of this great spirit was constrained to a single image, I felt disinterested. But when I began to see that this divinity pulses through everything, I realized – Spirit is all around us.

Divinity is mirrored in sacred geometry reflecting from melting glacial drops, and prisms of ice shimmering on mountain caps. This spark is in the moss resurrecting life atop the silt, the mycelium weaving patterns of existence, the quiet hum of wind through the trees.

Ancient codes instruct flowers to bloom, seeds to germinate, cycles to unfold with perfect precision. Consciousness rests within the tiniest seeds, orchestrating the continuity of life. Up to a thousand species of microbes live within each being, whispering the language of vitality.

The earth's ecosystems are rich tapestries, woven with intelligence and resilience. There are forests untouched by human hands, soil teeming with life, and ancient groves that have stood for centuries, breathing in symphony with the cosmos. Biodiversity enriches every inch of unspoiled land; just as divine presence fortifies every corner of existence.

The frequency of nature is immeasurable, just like the expansiveness of our Creator, the volume of our oceans, and the love we deserve. I have learned that what I admire most is the God I see in her, in you, in me. This life force exemplifies the potency of each meaningful connection and experience. How vibrant and lush this energy magnifies when we stop witnessing only what we are told to see – when we reclaim our sight and open our eyes with a sovereign lens.

One of my favorite authors, Bill Plotkin, teaches that *"we must remain uncorrupted even amid calamity and tragedy. We must show up fully, not attached to outcome, and be innocently present to the wonders of our world, unhampered by our socially acquired blinders and filters."*

This is an invitation – to step beyond the boundaries of conditioned perception, to explore the boundless presence that breathes through all things. The world outside the box awaits.

How We Pray

The conditions we are raised with construct the fibers of the web we spin in life. We are shaped by our environments, the narratives we inherit, and the beliefs we absorb. Many religious traditions teach us to pray for mercy, to seek forgiveness, to plead for what we desire. Prayer, though, is an act of attunement, and is not meant to be sourced from desperation. A prayer centered in clarity asks for discernment, for the wisdom to move in integrity, for the strength to remain aligned with truth.

When we use prayer only to ask for what we want, we risk disappointment, losing faith when our requests do not materialize. If we anchor our prayers in gratitude, they become an invocation of harmony. Do you take time each day to simply say *thank you* – to honor the breath that fills your lungs, the ground that carries you, the infinite intelligence guiding all things? Rather than seeking material gain, we can pray for guidance, for expansion, for remembrance of the divine within and all around us.

Richard Rudd, in *The Seven Sacred Seals*, describes prayer as *an intimate dialogue between self and the higher self*. The essence of prayer is selflessness, transparency, and the lifting of the heart. Prayer is about connection, not transactions. We have permission to speak with the Divine as we would a trusted companion, to share our dreams, our struggles, our joys. Sometimes prayer is not a request at all, but a check-in, a moment of presence with the sacred.

Before religion was structured, how did our ancestors pray? Before the birth of Christ, where were our prayers directed? This is an invitation to pray freely, beyond preconceptions, beyond boundaries. To feel the presence of spirit, to open the heart, to engage in genuine conversation. In African spirituality, prayers are not pleaded, they are commanded, affirmed with confidence, faith, and trust. We do not beg for what we need; we declare our requirements into being. We step into alignment and know that what is meant for us will come.

The hand that harms is also the hand that heals. Just as we choose how we move through the world; we choose how we pray. Are our prayers sowing peace, healing, and love, or are they reinforcing fear, division, and lack? Prayer is a force, not something that qualifies as being passive. We are referencing the sacred thread that weaves intention into reality.

Pray as often as breath allows. Pray with the trees, feeling their wisdom in your palms. Pray as you cultivate the earth, as you nourish yourself and others. Let your cooking be a prayer, your love resonate with prayer, your movement answer prayers. Allow your being to be a living hymn of gratitude and devotion.

Prayer for Awareness

I pray for the souls of the innocent, for the ones who cry in silence – the creatures caged, the rivers poisoned, the forests felled with trembling hands.

I pray not just for the animals suffering, but for the veins of this Earth, the pristine waters siphoned dry, the land bled of her plasma and marrow – being petroleum, the lifeblood stolen from beneath every enchanted region of this world.

I pray for the ancient ice that melts into memory, for the penguins and polar bears fading into ghosts before our very eyes. Let us learn to keep the carbon buried, to leave the sacred petroleum untouched, to cease this war on wonder.

The rainforests of Indonesia, Brazil, Malaysia, Peru are vanishing faster than we can speak their names. Entire ecosystems erased in minutes. I pray for Sumatran tigers, the orangutans, jaguars, sloths, and toucans, the life woven into green cathedrals now turned to ash.

I pray that we awaken – that we stop feeding addiction with the blood of the Earth. That we break free from flesh, release our grasp on factory farms, dismantle the machines that steal land for cattle, for the wheat and soy that fatten them, all while children starve in Cambodia, in the U.S., in Africa, in India, where food is currency, where survival is a lottery.

I pray for the trees, the elders of our world, that we stop seeing them as profit and start honoring them as kin. Each redwood, every cedar, the trembling aspen carries the weight of time, and yet, we cut them down for the luxury of wine, for the comfort of leather, for a fleeting indulgence that costs us everything.

I pray for the suffering of chickens, pigs, cows, horses, and lambs, who know only darkness before they are taken. Let us recognize that the soul is not ours to consume, that flesh does not belong on plates, that a life is never given willingly.

I pray for the Indigenous, for the tribes displaced, for the rivers once clear now tainted with crude. For the languages silenced, mothers lost, and the children left to wander where their ancestors once thrived.

I pray for the elephants, whose tusks are valued by man more than their breath. For the rhinos already lost, the whales choking on plastic, for the oceans trawled clean of life.

I pray for the rain to return, for the aquifers to heal, for the soil to be restored to a natural balance – untainted by pesticides and greed. I pray we learn to sustain ourselves without taking from the ocean, without poisoning the land, without watching the planet suffocate for the sake of convenience.

I pray we see through the illusions. That we stop worshiping biotech giants and return to the heirloom seeds of Gaia, letting mycelium weave magic through soil that was never meant to be drowned in chemicals.

I pray for a world where forests remain standing, where rivers run clear, where oceans breathe freely, where children inherit a land worth inheriting.

I pray we remember that peace is not found in prayers alone – but in action. May we act with love. May we move with wisdom. May we wake up soon.

Spiritual Sorcery

Embodied spirituality is when our connection with spirit becomes a lived practice. Prayer is a conduit of divine energy, a way to align with Source. The story of God is written through the purity of our hearts, the clarity of our actions. When we move in alignment, even if we do not immediately perceive how events are unfolding in our favor, we must trust in divine orchestration. What happens in our lives is happening *for* us, not *to* us. Our faith is revealed in the absence of fear. When we release all fear and fully surrender to divine protection, our connection strengthens, becoming unshakable.

Across the world, indigenous traditions carry unique perspectives on creation and the sacred forces that shape existence. From the legend of Skywoman descending upon Turtle Island to the countless deities that embody aspects of nature, the diversity of spiritual understanding is vast. No single religion can claim dominion over the universal frequency of prayer. The Divine is not bound by doctrine, nor confined to the image of a single being.

The idea that God only lived as one man – embodied in one form – mirrors the myth of human supremacy. Divine essence flows through all of creation, not only humankind. The savior is resurrected endlessly – in the eagle soaring above vast landscapes, in the wisdom of trees, in the delicate balance of microbial life. God is the breath of the jaguar, the whisper of the wind, the unfurling of a fern. Great Spirit dances on the wings of a hawk and rests on golden aspen leaves swaying in the autumn sun.

Divinity is energy, a frequency, a vast intelligence that is expressed through all life forms. This is the life force that instructs seeds to germinate, that orchestrates the harmony of ecosystems. Every step upon untouched forest soil is a communion with God, a reverence for the holiness within each atom of existence.

When we cultivate purity within ourselves – through thought, action, and nourishment – we provide a sacred terrain for divinity to expand within us. Impurities distance us from our highest potential as sovereign beings. Just as poisoned waters still carry energy, so too do all substances hold vibrational imprints. The difference lies in the intention behind their creation, their use, their consumption. Energy is neither good nor bad, the form is only altered by the wielded consciousness.

Frequency determines proximity. We are naturally drawn to energies that reflect our own vibration. Those who match our frequency feel familiar; those of higher resonance challenge us to rise. This is why the saying rings true: *your vibe attracts your tribe.* If all beings on Earth shared a unified rhythm, a collective song and dance, perhaps division would dissolve, replaced by harmony in movement and spirit.

Keeping the Sacred

When we have traveled up roads in life that teach the wisdom of silence, and across terrains that remind us of the freedom found in our breath, we begin to understand the sacredness within each moment. As we unravel from limiting beliefs, release from cultural conditioning, and step into our authentic state of being, we glorify the struggles that shaped us. Every encounter, whether welcome or resisted, has served a purpose in our evolution. This is divine orchestration.

With maturation, we learn to honor the temple of our body, paying homage to the sacredness of our cells, lungs, tissues, and vessels. We no longer see hills and mountains as resources to be extracted but as spiritual abodes, ancient sentinels of wisdom. We recognize that animals, plants, rocks, stars, and all forms of life are not separate from us but extensions of our energetic field, co-creators in this grand design.

Across cultures and traditions, those who sought wisdom understood that connection to the sacred required discipline, solitude, and reverence. In Andean Quechua traditions, seekers climbed to high-altitude mountains for Ayni rituals, fasting and communing with Pachamama (Mother Earth) to receive guidance before returning to their communities. The Yoruba of West Africa sent initiates into nature to meditate and fast, seeking wisdom from the Orishas before stepping into leadership.

In Japanese Zen Buddhism, monks undertook *sesshin*, rigorous silent meditation retreats to confront the depths of their being and sharpen their awareness. These practices reflect a universal truth – to strengthen one's connection to the divine, one must clear distractions, embrace stillness, and listen deeply.

To keep the sacred alive, one must embody the spirit of sacrosanctity in thought, words, and action. In ancient cultures, the land was not a resource to be exploited but a living entity, honored and protected. The Hopi saw their mesas as spiritual centers, just as the Māori revered their land as an ancestor.

The sacred has always been woven into daily life, not kept separate. Strengthening one's connection to Source means moving through the world with awareness, integrity, and reciprocity, ensuring that what is holy does not fade into abstraction but remains a guiding force, a presence, a way of being.

Abundance is scooped from abundance, and yet abundance remains. This is sacred reciprocity – the infinite flow of energy, the giving and receiving that maintains a delicate balance of existence. The more we pour into the wellspring of life with reverence, the more we are nourished in return.

When we tread gently upon the earth, when we offer gratitude before taking, when we align with the natural order, we strengthen our Source connection. In keeping the sacred, we honor the rhythm of creation. To strengthen our Source connection is to live in alignment with this great rhythm. To listen. To trust. To embody divinity in motion.

Mantras: The Pathway to Source

Mantras are ancient songs of the soul, syllables of power that carry the weight of intention and resonance of the universe. They are not mere words but vibrational keys, unlocking doors that separate the self from divine. To speak a mantra is to weave oneself into the cosmic rhythm, to remind the body, mind, and spirit of their sacred origin.

In every tradition where the mystical path is walked, mantras have been the foundation – a call to the unseen, a return to harmony. Sages knew that sound shapes reality, that words, when infused with pure intent, become forces of transformation. A mantra is both a declaration and a surrender. The whisper of the eternal into the finite, the tuning fork that aligns us with the great symphony of existence.

My three favorite mantras are:

I am empowered by everything.

I am eternal liberation.

I am enshrined in divine protection.

Resilience is an art, and a wing that can never be clipped. No matter how strong the wind, or heavy the rain, nothing impedes the flight. When we speak mantras with full conviction, we do not simply affirm what already is, we create space for what we call in.

A mantra can shape our reality as the river shapes the stone, as breath sustains the body. They are invocations that transcend time, reminding us that we are not separate from the force that moves tides, spins stars, and breathes life into the land. They bring us back to knowing, to clarity, to the unshakable presence of Source within.

Nourish With Cosmic Rays

In the soil resting beneath a giant tree, you will never find the ash, carbon, chlorophyll, minerals, or wood that are contained within the body of the tree and composition of leaves. There are elements in plants that never exist in soil. They are supplied by cosmic rays.

In human cells, there is no trace of the nutrients found in the food we eat. Only the gaseous and fluidous elements of what we ingest can enter the blood and assist in cellular regeneration. Therefore, we are not composed of what we eat; we are constituted with what we breathe and the residuum of our movement. Our cells are composed of cosmic rays, elemental essences that descend from the celestial bodies above.

We receive high levels of nourishment from being in nature where the air is pure, where our lungs expand, and where movement stimulates the circulation of our blood and lymph. We can go weeks without food, days without water, but breath is the essence of life. Without Prana, we cease to be.

A great teacher once shared that the lungs are the chief organs of digestion. Cosmic nitrogen nourishes tissues and vitalizes the body. Oxygen sustains the cells. Hydrogen moistens the lung surface and soothes the nerves. With each inhalation, oxygen flows into the blood, transforming the hue from dark to scarlet red. Each exhalation releases impurities, clearing the internal rivers of life.

With awareness, breathwork becomes a method of purification. Through fresh air and conscious breathing, we restore vitality and cleanse the body with the simplest and most powerful medicine – Prana, the breath of God. We must be mindful of the quality of air we breathe, as the air is no longer pristine.

Industrial pollutants, airborne toxins, and synthetic chemicals disrupt this sacred exchange. Smoke from corporate-ignited fires releases PM2.5 molecules that infiltrate our right to fresh air. Our respiratory epithelium, delicate and sacred, is under siege. Yet, through awareness, purification, and reverence for the breath, we reclaim our connection to Source.

Listen To Spirit

Spirit is always speaking, but are we listening? The language of Source is not always found in words, but in feeling, in alignment, in synchronicity. To strengthen our connection, we must partake only in what serves our highest good.

Forest bathing elevates the soul. Connecting with our companions and tribes uplifts us. Moving our bodies, eating purely, and praying with intention keeps our vibrations strong. Cleansing the body allows the soul to expand and grow within. Being with our children, present in the moment, reminds us of life's most profound joys. Using our gifts to bring light to others fills our cup and returns to us in ways unseen.

To listen to Spirit is to trust where we are guided. There will be times when we invest energy in a path that does not unfold as we intended. This is not failure, only a redirection. This is divine orchestration leading us where we are truly meant to be. We are not meant to control outcomes, only to be vessels of trust. We continue forward, anchored in goodness, surrendered to the higher plan.

Spiritual economics teaches us that we are sustained not by material wealth, but by the infinite wellspring of consciousness. The more we tap into this Source, the more we realize we are already abundant.

In *The Wind in the Willows*, the author writes, *"The river is a babbling procession of the best stories in the world, sent from the heart of Earth. What she does not have is not worth having, and what she does not know is not worth knowing."*

Like the river, Spirit flows unceasingly, whispering wisdom through the trees, the wind, the movement of the stars. We must quiet the noise that blocks our ability to hear her utterances, attune our hearts, and listen. This is how we receive confirmations that we are on the right path, leading in a good way.

God is Within: Strengthening Source Connection

If ever seeking a place to hide, know this – God has already chosen to reside within you. This is the last place we are conditioned to look yet is the only place where we will truly find divinity. When we outsource our sacredness, we create an empyrean disconnect, severing the bridge between our inner wisdom and the infinite intelligence that pulses through creation.

Just as corporations outsourcing labor disrupts the stability of local economies, so too does seeking externally what is already within leave us spiritually impoverished. The more we search outside ourselves for validation, healing, and truth, the further we drift from our sovereignty – from the ability to speak from our core, discern with clarity, and reclaim our natural role as healers, seekers, and seers.

This detachment stifles our capacity for truth, weakens our voice, and dulls the potency of our convictions. To step fully into our power, we must root ourselves in this inner knowing, ground into Source, and align with the rhythm of divine intelligence moving through us.

In testament, Yeshua reminds us, *"The kingdom of God does not come with observation; the kingdom of God is within you."* This is not a kingdom built of walls or bound by time – this refers to the sanctuary of the heart, an ever-present force, accessed through integrity, faith, and presence. To seek this sanctum outside is to wander, but to awaken here within is to arrive.

Albert Camus captures this truth in poetic form, offering a glimpse into the indomitable spirit that dwells within:

"In the midst of hate, there was within me, an invincible smile. During chaos, there was within me, an invincible calm. I realized that amid winter, there was within me an invincible summer, and this makes me happy. For this reveals that no matter how hard the world pushes against me, there is something stronger – something better – pushing right back."

This force within is God's unwavering presence, the essence that keeps us disciplined, persistent, and resilient. This is the divine principle, the root of strength and structure within our being.

What compels us to love in the face of hatred, to remain gentle amid brutality, to choose stillness when the world trembles, is this grand architect, the cosmic intelligence orchestrating all activity. When circumstances unravel, when tides shift unexpectedly, we do not break – we awaken.

This supreme current and primordial force keeps us composed while experiencing turbulence, resilient through hardships, and unshaken in the face of change. The celestial pulse is the breath between doubt and certainty, the fire between trial and triumph, the whisper that reminds us – God has never left.

The cosmic whisper is within. The spirit that moves through all things rests in our cells. The all-knowing presence is woven in strands of our DNA. The weaving force threads our body with our mind and spirit. When we choose to return, we remember that we were never lost.

Key Takeaways from Lesson V

Strengthening our connection to Source is not about seeking but about remembering.

Divine intelligence is not something external to be sought but an ever-present current flowing through all things.

The divine is woven into all things – our breath, the Earth, and the light within every cell.

We are never separate from divinity, only in need of remembrance.

Ancient traditions honored Source through prayer, reverence, and alignment with natural rhythms.

True prayer is an act of alignment, not of pleading or seeking outside of oneself.

Sound and vibration, such as Ohm, harmonize us with the frequency of creation.

We are nourished by forces beyond the visible – sunlight, breath, and cosmic wisdom.

Strengthening our connection to Source requires integration, stillness, and trust in divine orchestration.

God is not distant but an ever-present force moving through all life, guiding us home.

Whether through the resonant frequency of Ohm, the quiet dialogue of prayer, or the vibrational harmony of nature, our connection to Source is strengthened not by asking for what is outside of us but by embodying what has always been within.

Reflect and Apply Worksheet

1. Reflection on Divine Connection:

When have you felt most connected to Source in your life?

How do you personally define and experience the presence of divinity?

What practices currently help you strengthen this connection?

2. Releasing Separation:

Are there any beliefs or habits that make you feel separate from Source?

How can you begin to dissolve these illusions of separation?

What affirmations or mantras resonate with you to reinforce your unity with divine intelligence?

3. Prayer and Invocation:

What is your current relationship with prayer?

How does your approach to prayer shift when seen as an act of alignment rather than a request?

Write a personal invocation that affirms your connection to Source.

4. The Resonance of Sound:

Have you ever experienced the power of sound healing, chanting, or sacred music? Describe your experience.

How does sound influence your state of mind and energy?

What sounds in nature make you feel most at peace? How can you incorporate these into your daily life?

5. Embodiment of Source:

How can you live in a way that honors your divine connection?

What daily actions can you take to align more deeply with your soul's highest frequency?

Reflect on an area of your life where you can bring more reverence, awareness, or presence.

1. **Nature as a Teacher:**

How does spending time in nature enhance your spiritual awareness?

What elements of the natural world remind you of your connection to the divine?

Write a short reflection on a recent moment in nature where you felt aligned with something greater.

2. **Moving Forward:**

What commitments will you make to deepen your connection to Source?

How will you integrate the wisdom of this lesson into your daily practice?

What is one new habit or ritual you will adopt as a reminder of your ever-present connection?

Final Thought: Take a deep breath, place your hand on your heart, and affirm: *I am already home. I have never been separate. The way knows, and I trust in the unfolding of my divine path.*

This review and worksheet are designed to help you embody the teachings of *Strengthening Source Connection*, not just as knowledge but as a lived experience. May your journey be one of remembrance, alignment, and profound trust in the divine flow.

Lesson VI: Staying Out of Your Own Way

"The Great Way is not difficult for those who have no preferences. When love and hate are both absent, everything becomes clear and undisguised." — Sengcan, *Third Patriarch of Zen*

We are often the architects of our own obstacles. The divine current is always flowing, yet we stand in the path – clutching to our identities, attachments, fears, and illusions that prevent us from stepping fully into our essence. The greatest challenge is not external resistance but the self-imposed barriers we construct through unconscious habits, conditioned beliefs, and the clinging to that which no longer serves us.

The ancient masters understood this well – true wisdom is not attained through accumulation but through release. To unblock divinity, we must identify and surrender the patterns that keep us tethered to limitation. We must clear the channels through which the Great Way seeks to move.

Lao Tzu taught that, resistance to what is, creates suffering: *"Stop thinking and end your problems."* To stay out of our own way, we must first recognize how we obstruct our growth. Do we cling to doubt? Do we self-sabotage through fear or procrastination? Do we replay the same cycles, mistaking them for fate? Awareness is the first step to liberation.

Every addiction, habit, or vice that numbs our awareness or dulls our connection to Source siphons our life force. The Buddha spoke of attachment as the root of suffering – whether that attachment is to substances, distractions, unhealthy relationships, or self-destructive thoughts. True liberation comes when we reclaim our energy from the forces that deplete us.

The words we speak shape the world around us. Taoists remind us that those who speak too much lose their power – true wisdom moves in silence as much as in sound. To conserve our energy, we must discern when to offer our voice and when to simply be. Gossip, complaints, and reactionary speech scatter our power. A mindful tongue nourishes the soul.

To surrender blame is to reclaim sovereignty. When we accept that we are both the cause and the cure, we no longer wait for life to shift. We become recalibration. The Bhagavad Gita teaches: *"A person is made by their belief. As they believe, so they are."*

Taking responsibility for our thoughts, actions, and emotions means understanding that divinity flows best through a vessel that is open, clear, and aligned. To evolve, we must step aside, let go, and allow the wisdom of the universe to move through us. Release resistance. Dissolve attachment. Let the Great Way guide you.

Abstain From Glamorization

We rarely do well on pedestals. The air is thin at great heights, and illusions cast long shadows. The higher we are raised, the farther we must fall – not by our own missteps, but by the hands that once placed us there.

High expectations, when born from illusion, often lead to disillusionment. To be exalted as pristine is to be set up for desecration, for the world will hold a mirror to our humanity and call this reflection imperfection. Deification is often a doorway to disparagement.

To be lauded as impeccable and unblemished, then defiled and denounced for a minor defect or glitch is the cruel paradox of glorification. This is the essence of cancel culture, the cycle of aggrandizement and abandonment. One moment, we are the embodiment of greatness, the next, a fallen idol. But did we ever truly ascend, or was the illusion only theirs to shatter?

People script our lives in their minds, conjuring expectations built upon fantasy, mistaking admiration for ownership. They fashion roles for us, frames that do not fit, and when we refuse to conform to the portrait they have painted, they turn. They abhor what they once adored. When we step beyond their grasp, when we deny the reduction of our being to an image, we become the villain in their tale. To live on a pedestal is to become a prisoner to the expectations of those who place us there.

Yes, I hear that you adore me. You cherish the version of me that exists in your mind. You love the reflection of yourself you see in my existence. You worship me as a subordinate to your perception, a shimmering illusion to project your ideals on.

But I will not be reduced. I am not a relic to be displayed, nor an ornament to be praised. When I claim my own divinity, when I become the conductor of my own existence, suddenly the adoration fades. The moment I refuse to be a pawn in someone else's dream, I am cast aside, as if the reverence once held was nothing more than conditional devotion.

Let us neither worship nor seek to be worshipped. Let us neither idolize nor accept the weight of misplaced admiration. The path of truth is not paved with illusions, nor should we allow ourselves to be confined by another's expectation of greatness.

Raise the Average

What a blessing to exist in a body free from impurities, to move through life with impenetrable mental clarity, and to embody goodness as a guiding principle. The path of transformation is open to all, but requires intention, discipline, and the willingness to rise above the tides that seek to pull us under.

The law of averages teaches that we become the sum of the five most influential people in our lives. Their habits, their thoughts, their energy, whether expansive or diminishing, intertwine with our own. If we surround ourselves with stagnation, we risk sinking into mediocrity. If we allow ourselves to be tethered to those who resist growth, we may find our own wings clipped before flight.

To stay out of our own way, we must be mindful of the company we keep. If we sense a dissonance in our direction, we must examine our sphere of influence. Attracting a higher frequency of relationships requires a process of refinement – a shedding of old stories, attachments, and patterns that no longer align with our highest evolution. Growth demands that we release what no longer serves, even when comfort and familiarity tempt us to stay.

Yet, just as we are shaped by those around us, we must remember that we, too, shape others. We exist in the law of averages for those who place us in their top five. Each day, we hold the capacity to raise or lower the frequency of those we encounter. If we move aimlessly, content in mediocrity, we become another anchor, weighing down those who have the potential to soar. But if we rise, if we embody discipline, kindness, and wisdom, we lift those around us by the simple act of being.

To raise the average is to commit to excellence – not as a pursuit of perfection, but as a devotion to integrity, expansion, and light. This requires that we inspire those around us not by force, but by the undeniable radiance of a well-lived life. We embody the energy of evolution so completely that those who walk beside us feel compelled to ascend.

How can we commit, daily, to being an influence that elevates rather than stagnates? How can we ensure that our presence serves as a catalyst for transformation rather than a reinforcement of limitations? May we always seek to be the reason that others believe in their own capacity to grow. May we stay out of our own way, and in doing so, become a guiding force for those seeking to do the same.

Germinate the Seeds of Your Identity

There was a time when I was buried. Shackled in a system that sought to break me, confined for the mere possession of a plant that grows freely from the Earth. I spent years being tormented by the legal system. While incarcerated, I received letters – small reminders that the world outside had not forgotten me. One message, simple yet profound, stood out among the rest. This read: *They want to bury you, but you are a seed.*

Little gestures like this can make all the difference. I carried those words with me like a talisman, a reminder that no matter how deep the darkness, the seed does not fear the soil. Perhaps they want to bury us all. Perhaps, at times, we even bury ourselves – suffocating under self-doubt, false narratives, and the weight of expectations imposed upon us by a world that fears the uncontainable. We forget who we are. We neglect to honor the vivacity of our life force, the potency of our influence.

We might even dig the hole ourselves, letting others fill us with their corrupt interpretations of who we should be. We give them permission to define us, to weaken our resolve, to convince us we are not enough. We allow them to distract us with devices, false ideologies, and impurities that dull our inner light. Whoever *they* are is irrelevant. What matters is that we refuse to let this happen.

To break free, to push through the layers of imposed limitations, we must reclaim our sovereignty. When we rise, when we stretch toward the sun, we step into our power. We no longer welcome sabotaging spirits or weak influences into our orbit. We refuse to accept a narrative that minimizes our potential. We choose to align with the frequency of those who uplift, who challenge us to evolve, who honor our spirit rather than attempt to contain us.

I was always taught that if we do not stand for something, we will fall for anything. I have seen many falls. They fall for illusions of gold, for the comfort of stagnation, for a world that does not have their best interest at heart. Today, I stand.

I stand for good health. For sovereignty of spirit. For fathers' rights. For artists to find spaces where their voices can be heard. For children to know love, not just in words, but in the way their fathers show up for them in life. I stand so that others may one day find the strength to rise as well.

A seed does not grow into a tree overnight. The germinate must first break open, endure the darkness, and reach for something still unseen. We must also choose this path. The process is sacred. The unfolding is inevitable.

If we are patient, and we nurture the soil and honor the journey, we will one day stand tall – unshaken, unmovable, deeply rooted in the truth of who we are.

Obstruct the Obstacles

Life moves like a river – wild, unyielding, ever flowing. To surrender to the current is to trust, but to navigate well requires presence. We are smooth sailing until the raft collides with rocks, until we find ourselves funneled through narrow passages, with obstacles on all sides. Then we find our way through, arriving on the other side, wiser, stronger, shaped by the journey.

Adversity exists to refine us, not to break us. The wind against our back may shift, but change is the teacher. Resistance strengthens our resolve if we do not let the fear of hardship paralyze us. When we are tested, we are forged. When we remain steady amid the storm, we affirm our unshakable nature.

Thich Nhat Hanh once said, "*Smiling is very important. If we are not able to smile, then the world will not have peace. We do not bring about peace by going out for a demonstration against nuclear missiles. We make peace with our capacity of smiling, breathing, and being peace.*"

To smile through adversity, to breathe through discomfort, to move through struggles with grace – this is the path of mastery. Ascendancy is not avoidance or passive surrender. Embodying harmonic discipline is the ability to remain in our center when all else is designed to uproot us. Even when betrayed, even when falsely condemned, even when battling for what is just, we choose to stand steady.

The obstacles we encounter do not define us. Our response to them does. We can allow hardship to harden us, or we can become the river – fluid, flowing, unbreakable. In the face of difficulty, we smile, breathe, and manifest our justice, peace, and reunification. We choose how we respond to our encounters and experiences. Our decision reflects our character. May we always choose well.

Tame Your Demons

Learn to tame the demons, to nurture them, to remind them of their angelic nature. All darkness longs to reach light. Even night surrenders to dawn, even the seed buried in the black soil stretches toward the sun. If we resist this truth, we allow ourselves to be consumed by the very forces we are meant to transcend.

When a seed germinates, darkness is used as a catalyst for growth. Strength is gathered in the unseen, then breaks free from the shell of limitation. So too must we break free from the illusions that keep us bound – fear, doubt, anger, resentment. These are the parasites that can take hold if we let them, feeding off our energy, steering us toward self-destruction.

If we attract devils, entities, parasites, or sickness, this indicates that something in our energy field is asking to be transformed. Like stagnant water breeds disease, dormant emotions breed disharmony. If cancer develops in the body, this is an accumulation of trapped energy, undigested trauma, and xenobiotics the body could not purge. Cancer is not an enemy. The first step to healing is to understand, not fight, and listen to what the body, mind, and spirit are trying to express.

When we perceive our battles as something outside of us, we create separation. If we recognize that everything we encounter – light or dark – reflects something within, we regain our power. We do not destroy our demons; we transmute them. We lead them to light. We teach them, through love, that they no longer have a place within us.

To stay out of our own way, we must establish peace within. We must become the lighthouse rather than the lost ship. We must stand firm in the essence that we embody so that nothing parasitic can take root in our spirit. In doing so, we free ourselves, and we illuminate the path for others to do the same.

Call In Angels

There are moments on this path when we must call for assistance beyond what is seen, when the weight of the world threatens to pull us under, and we find ourselves seeking a light to illuminate the way. To stay out of our own way is to know when to surrender, and to recognize that we do not walk alone. Angels, guides, and ancestral spirits – these forces wait for us to invoke them, to call upon the unseen hands that steady us as we rise.

We are not here to struggle alone, or to fight the currents without aid. There is wisdom in knowing when to reach out, when to allow unseen forces to lift us, to guide our steps when the road is unclear. When we align with Source, when we humble ourselves enough to receive, we become vessels for divine orchestration.

I pray for those who transformed their microbiome to be no longer compatible with mine, that one day our paths will again align. I hold love for the shadows and affirm, with time, that darkness will find a way to shine. After chaos subsides, we remember all is divine. I ask spirit to bless me with a light that frees me to transcend to greater heights. Low frequencies are no match for my vibration. I call in angels to elevate my rise.

We must trust that what has left us was never truly ours, and what returns is meant to be. We honor the cycle of relationships, of grief, of transformation. Just as fallen leaves nourish the soil for new life, so too do our trials prepare the ground for what is to come. Flowers bloom where fallen leaves died. Floods from monsoons eventually dry. Ancient tears from indigenous lineages revivify the soil where tall trees now wait to be climbed. The caged bird spreads her wings again in a new life and leaves the past behind.

To stay out of our own way, we must release resistance, allow divine timing to unfold, and trust that angels walk with us, even in the shadows. We must be willing to break cycles, clear stagnation, and to call in healing beyond what we can imagine for ourselves.

I invoke all traumas to be broken and for my closed spirit to be pried back open. May love's wizardry regenerate the vessels of my shattered heart, so I can smile without the pain of my trials and emanate the goodness I foster through my dharma. I clear lifetimes of universal karma.

The assistance we are seeking is already here, waiting for our invitation. Let us call in angels, let us step out of the way, and let light lead us home.

Clearing the Path to Freedom

Healing begins in the mind. Before the body can be restored, before the spirit can break free, the mind must be cleared of obstructions. Doubt lingers in caverns of hesitation, hiding in the dark corners where fear takes root. If the mind is cured, the body follows, and the soul is unshackled from the weight once carried.

I cure my mind from the doubt that hides out in caves, where obstacles cannot be surmounted. When my sight drowns in unforgiving waves, I ask to be resuscitated back to life in the stillness of calm seas.

The mind is both architect and destroyer, creator and saboteur. When left unchecked, illusions are manufactured, barriers where none exist are created, and we experience suffering where there is only transformation. When trained, and when cultivated with care, the mind becomes the great liberator. We must be willing to relinquish what no longer serves, to detach from the illusions that bind us, so that we may truly heal.

I seek courage to live void of fear, unattached to what I am required to release so I can heal. My career will always be honoring what my soul feels. I choose which spokes move my medicine wheel. To stay out of our own way, we must remove the weights that tether us to stagnation. The illusions of unworthiness, of failure, of limitation – these are mirages. The moment we dissolve them, we free ourselves to move forward, unburdened.

Every thought we cultivate, every belief we allow to take root, shapes the reality we step into. Let those thoughts be infused with wisdom. Let the mind be a field of clarity, not confusion.

I manifest illusory views dissolving into sweet nectars of what is alive for me and real. May I be blessed with a gentleness that is ethereal. Measure my steps with finesse. Undress my hardships and reconnect my freedom with nakedness. Erase ignorance and bring back the elements of my innocence.

To cure the mind is to take authority over our own thoughts, to choose expansion over contraction, to breathe wisdom into every decision. This describes the process of breaking free from conditioning, returning to our essence, and refusing to let external forces dictate our internal peace. The mind, when properly aligned, becomes the gateway to all healing.

Breathe out cynicism and inhale primordial wisdom. Find rhythm with patience and precision. When I write down my goals, stand me up and force me to go get them. Empower me to conquer my demons as I refuse to engage with oblivion. Guide me, to dream awake, channeling worthiness through every meridian.

To heal the body, free the mind. To free the mind, return to truth. In doing so, we step into the boundless space of possibility, where the past no longer dictates the future, and the spirit is free to move as always meant to – unrestricted, unbreakable, infinite.

Reclaiming Inner Authority

To stay out of our own way, we must reclaim our sovereignty. This is a state of being, not just a word. A declaration that our spirit bows to no external force, that our choices belong to us, and that our path is ours to walk, unchained by the constructs of control, conditioning, or fear.

Sovereignty is self-possession, the unwavering embodiment of personal truth. We are required to know who we are at our core and refuse to be swayed by influences that seek to dilute or manipulate our essence. To be sovereign is to think freely, to move intentionally, and to govern our own being with wisdom and integrity.

The world is designed to sway us, pull us from our knowing, and convince us that our power is conditional – a power that must be granted by authority, by approval, by permission. The sovereign knows better. A sovereign being recognizes that true power cannot be taken away and does not come from external validation.

To reclaim sovereignty, we must first break free from the narratives that keep us bound. We must unlearn the programming that tells us we are small, unworthy, or incapable. We must dismantle the illusions of dependency, the falsehoods that tell us we must seek outside ourselves for truth, for healing, for permission to exist fully.

Sovereignty is alignment. This is the ability to discern what is ours to carry and what is not. We learn when to stand firm and when to release, when to speak and when to listen, when to walk away and when to build. This is the quiet confidence of a soul that has been met fully and refuses to be anything less than authentic.

We stay out of our own way by standing in this knowing. By refusing to give our power away. By honoring our autonomy, our choices, our freedom. Sovereignty is remembrance, not rebellion. The act of reclaiming what has always been ours. A sovereign being does not seek permission to shine. A sovereign being does not ask to be free. A sovereign being is free, simply by existing in truth.

Surrendering to the Flow

To stay out of our own way, we must learn to accept that all things are unfolding according to divine order. Acceptance means understanding the rhythm of life and choosing to move with the flow. The river always flows, trusting the destination ahead, and not resisting the course being carved.

As Eckhart Tolle reminds us, *"Whatever the present moment contains, accept as if chosen."* This perspective does not bind us to stagnation but liberates us from suffering. We cease to struggle against what is, and in doing so, we open ourselves to transformation.

In Native American traditions, acceptance was reverence, not merely tolerance. All were welcomed into the tribe, regardless of past hardships, lineage, or circumstance. Many of their legends remind us that the ones who were once outsiders – the orphaned, the lost, the rejected – often became the ones who saved the village. When we accept others, we create the conditions for healing, growth, and unity. When we accept ourselves, we create the conditions for peace.

The Serenity Prayer teaches us to seek the wisdom to know the difference between what we can change and what we cannot. We are now invited to summon the courage to change what we cannot accept. We must recognize the balance – between surrender and action, between stillness and movement. We do not resist the flow of life, but neither do we remain passive in the face of injustice.

As life unfolds, we learn that even hardships serve a purpose. The loss of a relationship is a clearing for something greater. The job that slips away is a redirection toward purpose. The obstacles are not blockages; they are detours guiding us to exactly where we are meant to be.

Acceptance means recognizing that every moment – whether joyous or painful – is a step on the path of divine unfolding. We trust in the process, have faith in the unseen, and maintain an unwavering knowing that everything is happening *for* us, never *to* us. As we breathe, let go, and surrender to the grand orchestration of life, we liberate ourselves from suffering and walk forward in alignment. Acceptance is the key that unlocks the door to freedom.

Reminder To Self

Keep walking the way you do. Court higher harmonies with every step. I see you. There is wisdom in the way you rise, again and again, from the depths where others may have surrendered. I have watched you hit rock bottom, and I honor the way you ascend – each fall refining your resilience, each hardship forging your strength. The trials were meant to break you, yet here you stand, not just intact, but transformed.

The incarceration, the injections, the starvation, the poisoning – each test was designed to determine your will. But your spirit is immutable. You have faced what would have shattered others, and yet, you emerged not bitter but enlightened. To stay out of your own way, remember this: you are unshaken. You are guided. You are exactly where you need to be.

I honor how you have become the parent you always needed as a child. You always show up, no matter what the conditions. You make memories while staying true to yourself. That is love.

Lao Tzu teaches, *"When you let go of what you are, you become what you might be."* Never forget, you are worthy, you are strong, and you are free from all your wrongs. Each new day is a renewal, a chance to refine your being, a moment to rise unburdened.

You humble yourself before the elders, the children, and the animals. You kneel to meet them where they are, knowing they hold wisdom beyond words. You listen, you learn, you honor.

I am with you when you pray with your ancestors, when you call upon your warriors for guidance and support. I sense your devotion as you hug the trees, press your lips to their bark, and taste the potency of their sap, absorbing the life force that flows through their ancient veins.

You keep your body pure, plant-based, energetically clear. I thank you for leaving your footprint gently, for moving through the world with mindfulness, for touching Earth with grace.

If ever you are placed on a pedestal, you step down, ensuring you walk beside, never above, your brothers. You do not seek hierarchy; you seek unity. The way you live is an offering.

I appreciate how you express gratitude for the abundance in your life. Gratitude is the bridge to infinite blessings, the key to keeping the path clear.

Stay humble. Remain steady. Keep going.

The way knows.

The Illusion of Superiority

To stay out of our own way, we must dissolve the illusion of superiority, the belief that elevating oneself above others is a path to fulfillment. The truth is no one is made greater by the suppression of another. Superiority complexes arise not from genuine strength, but from insecurity, from the fear that another's light may outshine one's own. True power moves with grace, with wisdom, and with an understanding that all beings have a place within the sacred design of existence. This does not necessitate a need to control, diminish, or compete.

History has shown us that when fear takes hold, this manifests as division, as the attempt to dominate rather than coexist. Across time and cultures, systems of oppression have been fueled by the deep-seated anxiety that another's excellence is a threat rather than a testament to human potential. The wise understand that one's brilliance does not diminish another's but rather serves as an invitation for all to rise.

Jealousy and competition are illusions that bind us to suffering. As the Bhagavad Gita teaches, *"Those who are free from selfish attachments and whose minds are fixed in wisdom are free from envy and fear."* When we release the need to compare, prove, dominate, we free ourselves from measuring our worth against another's.

The true path is one of harmony, of lifting one another, of recognizing that sovereignty does not mean separation but alignment with the natural flow of life. We acknowledge our own gifts without seeking to diminish the gifts of others.

If we are to walk in a good way, we must relinquish the false narratives of superiority, division, and competition. We must remember that true greatness is not found in hierarchy but in humility. The one who truly knows himself has no need to prove himself. The one who is at peace has no need to conquer. The one who understands his divine nature seeks not to rule, but to uplift.

Eluding Patterns

Richard Rudd writes in *Gene Keys*, *"When you raise the frequency beyond the reach of concepts such as success and failure, you remember that all of life moves in a great cosmic pattern. As you let go into this pattern, you always find your natural support within."* To stay out of our own way, we must recognize when we are trapped in cycles that do not serve us. The key to breaking patterns is elevation.

To elevate, we must first observe. What depletes us? What drains our energy? What habits, thoughts, or relationships keep us tethered to stagnation? Much of what binds us is illusion – scarcity mindsets, fears passed down through generations, comfort in the familiar, even when the familiar keeps us small.

Lao Tzu reminds us, *"Watch your thoughts; they will become your words. Watch your words; they will become your actions. Watch your actions; they will become your habits. Watch your habits; they will become your destiny."* The life we live is the result of the patterns we follow. To shift our reality, we must shift our frequency.

What we consume – mentally, emotionally, physically – either raises or lowers our vibration. The dependence on artificial substances, processed foods, and synthetic distractions weakens our clarity and dulls our spirit. To break free, we must return to nature. We must align ourselves with what is real, what nourishes, what strengthens.

To stay out of our own way, we must stop feeding cycles that are not ours to perpetuate. What lifestyle habits or limiting thought patterns hold you back from raising your frequency beyond the reach of concepts such as success and failure? The moment we recognize them; we gain the power to break free. When we do, we remember. We are not meant to repeat the past. Our intent is to transcend all past experiences into ways of empowerment.

Stay out of your own way. Do not allow the mirage of superiority to block the blessings meant for you. Walk in wisdom. Walk in reverence. Walk in truth. The way knows.

Key Takeaways from Lesson VI

Glamorization is a trap. To be placed on a pedestal is to be confined to others' expectations. True power is not in idolization but in authenticity.

The law of averages impacts us. We become the sum of the five most influential people in our lives. Surrounding ourselves with those who elevate rather than diminish is essential.

We are seeds, not victims. Adversity is meant to germinate our growth, not bury us. To rise, we must first break free from false narratives that confine us.

Obstacles refine us. Just as a river carves a path through stone, we are shaped by the challenges we navigate. Adversity is not a signal to stop but an invitation to flow.

Demons are meant to be transmuted, not feared. The shadows we face exist not to destroy us but to be guided toward light. We do not fight darkness; we transform.

Angels and guidance are available. We are never alone on this journey. When we align with Source, we call in higher frequencies to support our ascent.

Healing begins with the mind. Before the body can be restored, the mind must be freed from doubt, fear, and illusion. Clear thinking leads to clear living.

Sovereignty is our birthright. No external force grants or removes our freedom that is inherent. To be sovereign is to govern oneself with integrity and wisdom.

Acceptance is not passivity. To surrender to the flow of life is not to give up but to move with divine orchestration.

Patterns must be transcended. The cycles we repeat shape our destiny. When we recognize and break limiting habits, we elevate beyond the reach of failure and success.

Reflect & Apply Worksheet

1. Identifying Self-Imposed Barriers

What habits, thoughts, or beliefs do you recognize as obstacles in your life?

How do these limitations manifest in your daily experiences?

What is one thing you can release today to create more space for growth?

2. Evaluating Your Sphere of Influence

Who are the five most influential people in your life?

Do they elevate your frequency or tether you to stagnation?

What steps can you take to surround yourself with individuals who inspire growth and wisdom?

3. The Pedestal Trap

Have you ever placed someone on a pedestal, only to be disappointed when they revealed their humanity?

Have you ever felt pressured to maintain an image that does not fully represent you?

How can you cultivate relationships that honor authenticity rather than illusion?

4. Transmuting Obstacles into Strength

Reflect on a past hardship that ultimately led to your growth. How did this refine you?

What current obstacle can you shift your perspective on to see as an opportunity for transformation?

How can you apply the wisdom of the river – flowing rather than resisting – to a challenge in your life?

5. Calling in Guidance

In moments of uncertainty, how do you seek support from divine or ancestral forces?

What is one way you can deepen your connection with the unseen guidance that surrounds you?

Write a personal invocation or prayer to call in higher wisdom and protection.

6. Breaking Patterns & Releasing Attachments

Are there repetitive cycles in your life that no longer serve you?

What thoughts or behaviors do you recognize as conditioning rather than truth?

How can you consciously shift your energy toward alignment with your highest self?

7. Embodying Sovereignty

What does sovereignty mean to you?

Where in your life do you still give away your power, and how can you reclaim what you have lost?

How can you practice radical self-governance while still remaining open to divine flow?

8. Acceptance & Surrender

What is something you are currently resisting in your life?

How might acceptance of this situation free you rather than hinder you?

In what ways can you remind yourself daily to trust in divine orchestration?

Closing Affirmation:

Take a deep breath, place your hand on your heart, and affirm:

I surrender all resistance. I move with the divine current, not against the force. I trust in the unfolding of my highest path. I am exactly where I need to be.

Lesson VII: Trusting Divine Orchestration

"Once you make a decision, the universe conspires to bring this to fruition."

Throughout time and across civilizations, those who have walked the sacred path have spoken of a force greater than human will, a current that moves through life with perfect precision, arranging events beyond our immediate understanding. This force – whether called Tao, Dharma, Fate, or the Hand of God – is divine orchestration.

To trust divine orchestration is to surrender to the rhythm of existence, knowing that every experience – whether a delay, encounter, or trial – is an essential note in the symphony of our unfolding. We learn to have faith in divine timing.

Lao Tzu, the sage of Taoism, taught: *"Nature does not hurry, yet everything is accomplished."* This wisdom reminds us that all things arrive in their appointed season – the seed is not forced into bloom, nor does the river resist the mountain. Life unfolds as curated. In trusting divine timing, we release the urgency of control and allow the universe to work in ways we may not yet see.

The ancients watched the stars, the birds, the patterns of the wind, believing that messages from the divine were always present. Lakota people say: *"The universe is talking to us, we just have to learn how to listen."* Synchronicities – those moments where everything aligns too perfectly to be coincidence – are signposts of divine orchestration. A chance encounter, a repeated number, a song that plays at just the right time – these are whispers from the unseen, guiding us toward where we are meant to be.

Resistance delays our path. In Hindu philosophy, karma is not punishment, but correction. When we resist what is meant for us, we create friction between our desires and the flow of the universe. The more we struggle against change, loss, or uncertainty, the longer we remain entangled in cycles of suffering.

The Bhagavad Gita reminds us: *"You have the right to work, but never to the fruit of work. Let not the rewards of action be your motive, nor be attached to inaction."*

To move forward, we must release attachment to the outcome, knowing that even setbacks are simply redirections leading us to something far greater than we imagined. We surrender control while staying engaged in life. To trust divine orchestration is to dance with life instead of struggling in opposition to what has been arranged.

The Hopi people have a prophecy that says: *"There is a river flowing now very fast. So great and swift that there are those who will be afraid. They will try to hold on to the shore. Know the river has a destination. We must let go of the shore, push off into the middle of the river, keep our eyes open, and our heads above the water."*

Surrender is stepping fully into trust, knowing we are always protected, always guided, always carried. When we stop grasping, when we release fear, when we trust that every twist in the path is leading us exactly where we need to go – we align with the divine order that has been holding us all along.

Trust the timing. Recognize the signs. Let go of resistance. Know that the universe is conspiring in your favor.

Being Unafraid

The warrior's path is not paved with the absence of fear but with a deep willingness to meet fear as an ally. To be unafraid is not to exist without trembling but to walk forward, eyes wide, embracing the unknown as the sacred terrain of evolution. As Chögyam Trungpa teaches, *"The basis of warriorship is being unafraid of who you are. A definition of bravery is accepting yourself."* This is the art of genuine embodiment – standing unguarded in the presence of all that emerges within and around us.

A river does not resist the stone, nor does the wind beg for permission to move through the trees. The natural world models the deepest form of courage – full participation in the unfolding of existence. Trees do not withhold the offering of leaves when autumn calls, nor does the eagle hesitate to trust the current that lifts strong wings to the sky. Fear is merely a signal that something is knocking on the door of transformation.

To armor oneself against the lessons carried in these moments is to reject the very guidance being sought. Indigenous traditions speak of the strength found in circles – where wisdom flows freely, held by the rhythm of voices uniting in truth. A gathering of men and women, each one stripping away pretense, allows for the weaving of collective strength.

Vulnerability becomes a doorway, not a weakness, and through shared stories, laughter, and ritual, the old wounds of separation dissolve. The Lakota speak of *Mitákuye Oyás'iŋ* – all are related. The healing of one is the healing of all.

True warriors are not those who build fortresses of control but those who stand undefended, allowing life to move through them unfiltered. The great ones, the wisdom keepers, the masters whose names echo through time, were not guarded or rigid – they were fluid, surrendered, and deeply attuned to the pulse of existence. Their power was born from alignment, not resistance.

A commitment to truth shapes destiny. The pull of what is desired will create the pathway necessary, but one must be willing to step. To return to the elemental forces is to return to attunement. Take off the shoes. Let the earth speak. Seek answers from the river's reflection rather than the artificial glow of a screen. The knowing one seeks is embedded in the roots, the winds, the firelight of the ancestors who whisper guidance in the quiet spaces between thoughts.

Energy is neither created nor destroyed, only directed. A life lived in the suppression of one's brilliance is a life spent exhausting vital force. If anger or fear rises, honor this as a sacred flare – a call to realignment, a moment of pause where the map can be recalibrated. To adjust is to reclaim authority over one's destiny.

These moments of reckoning, of shadow work, of deep listening, are the gateways to evolution. The weaving of the feminine and masculine, the bridging of what was fragmented, the restoration of inner harmony – this is the work. The imprint of truth, when studied with sincerity, becomes more revelatory than the truth itself. As Rumi reminds, *"Do not be satisfied with the stories that come before you. Unfold your own myth."* Trust the unfolding.

Merlin's Magic

Magic is the breath of the cosmos made visible; the whisper of the unseen woven into the fabric of the manifest world. The sorcerer does not force the miraculous but aligns with the rhythm of the sacred, allowing the currents of creation to flow unimpeded. Merlin, the great alchemist of legend, was not merely a man but a conduit – an embodiment of the universal spirit moving through time, bending reality toward harmony as those who sought truth stepped into divine alignment.

Love is the highest frequency of enchantment, the resonance through which miracles unfurl. Magic is not an illusion, nor a trick to deceive the senses, but the ancient force that shapes worlds – the same unseen power that beckons seeds toward the sun and calls the tides to rise and fall in celestial synchrony. The elders teach that prayers, songs, and ancestral invocations are the true sorcery of the soul, each word a vessel carrying intention into the vast field of possibility.

Earth herself is the grand magician. Look at the mycelial networks beneath the forest floor – silent, unseen, yet orchestrating the great symphony of life. Paul Stamets speaks of fungi as the *"earth's natural internet,"* a web of intelligence that nourishes, communicates, and transforms decay into new vitality. What was once rock and barren silt, left in the wake of ancient glaciers, is soon embraced by the soft tendrils of mycelium, birthing moss, then flowers, then towering trees. What once seemed lifeless is restored, not by force but through the patient, unbreakable dance of nature's alchemy.

So too does the sorcerer transform. To become an agent of divine magic is to weave oneself into the grand design, to recognize the golden threads binding all living things. This sacred connection is the essence of true magic, a knowing that life is not meant to be controlled but danced with, not dominated but co-created. The domesticated mind, severed from the roots of ancestral knowing, has forgotten this. But the wisdom keepers of old remind us: the cure for disconnection is remembrance.

We are invited to reindigenize, to reclaim the rhythms of the land, to listen once more to the wisdom of wind and water, to trust the great unfolding. When we choose to walk in reverence, we become the architects of a new reality, the ones who call forth what is waiting to be revealed.

Those who honor the path of the magician do not conform to the boxes drawn by artificial constructs. The mind untethered ascends, moving beyond the rigid walls of limitation into the constellations of expanded thought. The story-singer, the wisdom-keeper, the artist whose hands shape the formless into beauty – each is a channel through which magic flows, each a participant in the symphony of creation.

There is no distance between the divine and Earthly. Those who walk with open hearts recognize divinity in the smallest of moments – the birth of a child, the song of a morning bird, the hush of snowfall blanketing the mountains. This is the call: to see with new eyes, to embrace the unseen forces that have always guided the way.

Merlin's magic is not a relic of forgotten myths but a living force, awaiting those who choose to step into the current of universal flow. The invitation is clear – dissolve the illusion of separation, reclaim the birthright of connection, and surrender to the sacred dance of divine orchestration.

Revivification of Magic

"We all start out knowing magic."

A child comes into this world unburdened, still tethered to the great mystery, eyes wide with wonder, hands eager to touch the pulse of creation. Before the weight of conditioning molds perception into narrow corridors, there is only the infinite, the unfiltered connection to spirit, to the sacred forces that weave existence. The revival of magic is a remembering of what has always been, not a summoning of something lost.

To walk the path of trust in divine orchestration, one must look to the children – the untouched wisdom keepers who have not yet forgotten. They dance without asking permission, laugh without reason, and speak to trees without doubt. Their connection to spirit has not been severed by logic's rigid grip. In their presence, we are called to return to the essence we once embodied, the state before skepticism veiled the miraculous.

Wisdom urges us: let the children awaken what has long been suppressed. Let their wildness remind us of our own untamed nature, their joy rekindle the light we buried beneath years of expectation and constraint. Let them be free – not shaped by the antiquated fears we inherited, nor restrained by the smallness of minds that forgot how vast existence truly is.

Education, when wielded with reverence, should not be confined but should expand. The young ones are not meant to be filled with limitations disguised as knowledge, nor weighed down by doctrines that imprison the spirit. Rather, let their learning be an exploration – one that nourishes the senses, deepens the soul's inquiry, and encourages the discovery of what brings life, wonder, and belonging.

To guide them toward the divine is not to hand them a map but to let them find their own way into the mystery. The spirit of God, of the universal force is felt in the wind's whisper, in the way fire crackles in the night, in the unseen hands that orchestrate serendipity. The force of creation does not belong to any singular name or doctrine. Let kids ask, let them wonder, let them forge their own sacred communion without our fears distorting the path.

In doing so, we become stewards of their magic, guardians of their boundless spirits. We encourage them to run barefoot through the fields we never allowed ourselves to roam. We invite them to climb trees, to sing to the rivers, to create with abandon. We make space for their laughter, their play, their unfiltered expression – realizing, in doing so, that we are not merely guiding them; they are leading us home.

This is the generation rising with us, not behind us. They arrive with wisdom beyond their years, clarity untainted by the wounds of the past. They come to show us where we faltered, to illuminate the fractures in our ways of being, and to remind us of the responsibility we hold in mending what was broken. The cycle of neglect, of unconscious repetition, must not continue. The mindless perpetuation of ignorance is no longer an option.

We heal our lineage not by imposing our burdens upon them but by choosing to be for them what we once needed. We step aside so they may step forward, and in doing so, we rediscover the magic we once thought was lost. We remember, at last, the meaning of trusting the unfolding, surrendering to the great orchestration, returning to the mystery with open arms.

Visual Dysbiosis: Disconnection from Sacred Sight

Dysbiosis is life out of harmony, a disruption in the sacred balance that governs all living systems. Most speak of this condition in relation to the unseen world of microbes – the living intelligence of the gut, the skin, the very fabric of the human form, but the fracturing of balance does not begin in the body alone. The eyes, too, suffer when perception is misaligned.

Vision is more than sight. The lens through which life is witnessed determines the landscape of reality. When the spirit resists the unfolding, when trust in divine orchestration wavers, the field of vision distorts. Clarity dims. Awareness narrows. The eyes may open each morning, yet the view remains constrained by self-imposed limitations. This is *visual dysbiosis* – a crisis of perception, a warping of sight that blinds the beholder to the vastness of the path before them.

Like an ecosystem stripped of biodiversity, where once-thriving rivers run dry and forests stand bare, a mind unwilling to trust the sacred unfolding becomes barren. When belief in life's inherent guidance withers, the ability to see the signs – the synchronicities, the invitations, the whispered revelations – fades. The universe is always speaking, but misalignment muffles the call.

The ancients knew that true vision required purification, clearing the inner lens before the outer world could be seen truly. The mystics did not seek to conquer sight, but to refine perception – to allow clarity to emerge as a reflection of inner harmony.

When vision is clouded by resistance, the world appears hostile. Everything seems unjust, unkind, unmovable. Yet, the moment the inner terrain shifts, the landscape changes. What once seemed impossible becomes clear. What once appeared as misfortune is revealed as guidance.

Visual dysbiosis is a form of exile from the living truth, a symptom of distrust, a refusal to surrender to the rhythm that has been orchestrating every heartbeat, every sunrise, every convergence of souls. The remedy is not to force clarity but to soften into alignment.

Healing begins with reconnection. The body does not restore balance through force, but through gentle return – through nourishment, rhythm, and honoring the wisdom of the cloaked world that exists within. So too must the eyes reorient – not by straining to see, but by relaxing into trust.

One who walks in harmony with divine orchestration sees through the eyes of the hawk – perception broad, awareness keen. The shifting patterns of life do not appear as obstacles, but as movements in the great unfolding.

To heal the vision, one must first heal the trust. The hands of the cosmos have never failed to guide. The path has always been laid with precision. But sight must be cultivated, like the soil before planting, like the breath before song.

Trust, and the world expands. Surrender, and the signs become clear. Open the inner eye, and witness the great design being revealed, as she always has, as he always will.

Regenerating Wholeness: A Return to Sovereignty

The sacred path demands surrender. Not the kind that weakens or diminishes, but the surrender that dissolves resistance, allowing the divine current to flow unimpeded through every aspect of existence. For so long, a weight unseen has pressed upon the spirit. The self has been restrained, held back from stepping fully into the grand design that has always awaited. But the moment arrives – a reckoning, an unshackling.

In the presence of those who stand in truth, bearing witness to the unraveling of all that no longer serves, a great release is set into motion. Vulnerability, when embraced, is a gateway. In the center of a sacred circle, surrounded by those who hold space with unwavering presence, the remnants of old identities fall away. Stagnant energy, patterns of contraction, unnecessary shame – dissolve like mist under the rising sun. What remains is a being unburdened, stripped of illusion, standing in the rawness of authenticity.

Letting go is not a loss but an act of devotion to the unfolding path. Love, in truest form, is never possessed. When one departs, choosing another direction, the separation is not a mistake, not a wound inflicted by fate, but an act of divine orchestration, a movement designed by forces far beyond the mind's comprehension. To resist is to strain against the inevitable, but to trust is to align with the current that has already carried the soul exactly where intended to be.

Healing is an act of regeneration, not a passive process. This is a conscious decision to return to wholeness. The heart, though stretched by grief, expands in the breaking. The wound is not a finality, but a portal to greater capacity. Love, ever-present, moves through all things – waiting to be received, waiting to be recognized in the spaces where one once believed absence resided.

Sovereignty is not a state given; this must be reclaimed. Breath is recalibrated. Movement is corrected. The body, once weighed down by ghosts of the past, walks forward unaccompanied by what once lingered. Solitude is no longer emptiness, but a liberation, a reclamation of worth.

To elevate beyond suffering is to transmute, not deny or suppress. In the fire of transformation, struggle melts. The heat burns away attachments to pain, the sweat that pours from the skin merges with the earth, and the old self crumbles, making way for a being who has stepped beyond limitation.

The ancient ones knew – true evolution is not in clinging to comfort, but in facing the flame, standing in the heat of purification until the form that emerges is one sculpted by divinity. In Buddhist teachings, transcendence comes through the mind. In the wisdom of native traditions, transcendence is through emotion, through feeling, through allowing the deepest currents of experience to move freely, unblocked.

This is the path of trust. A surrender into something far greater than the small self that once grasped for control. The orchestration has always been in place, the alignment never broken – only veiled.

To stand in gratitude for the unfolding, for the stripping away, for the lessons that burned yet revealed the deeper truth beneath, is to walk in harmony with the great mystery. The moment arrives. The veil lifts. The vision clears. The soul stands whole once more.

Thank you. Thank you. Thank you.

Key Takeaways from Lesson VII

The Symphony of Divine Orchestration

Every experience, whether joyous or challenging, is part of a greater divine plan.

Faith in divine timing requires patience, trust, and surrender.

Synchronicities serve as signposts, guiding us along the path meant for us.

Resistance creates suffering, while trust allows for fluid movement through life's transitions.

Being Unafraid

Courage is the ability to walk forward despite the presence of fear.

Vulnerability is a gateway to transformation.

The natural world models the surrender necessary for true alignment.

The warrior's path requires openness, authenticity, and trust in the unfolding.

Merlin's Magic & Revivification of Magic

Magic is not an illusion but the unseen forces shaping reality.

The interconnectedness of all living things allows for divine energy to flow.

Children remind us of the magic we once knew – rekindling wonder and possibility.

The cure for disconnection is remembrance and reverence for ancestral wisdom.

Visual Dysbiosis: Misalignment of Perception

When we resist divine orchestration, our perception distorts, and clarity dims.

Trust in divine timing allows for expanded vision and alignment with purpose.

Healing the inner vision is key to recognizing the sacred design of life.

Regenerating Wholeness

Releasing past wounds and attachments allows for transformation.

Healing is an act of regeneration – sovereignty is reclaimed, not granted.

True surrender leads to alignment with divine intelligence.

Gratitude is the final stage of trust – acknowledging the unfolding of divine orchestration.

Reflect & Apply Worksheet

1. Observing Divine Orchestration in Your Life:

Describe a moment when everything seemed to align perfectly for you.

What signs or synchronicities have appeared recently that may indicate divine guidance?

Where in your life do you notice resistance? How might surrender create ease?

2. Embodying Fearlessness:

What fears have been holding you back from stepping fully into your path?

How can you honor these fears while still choosing to move forward?

Write a declaration of courage – what truth will you stand in without hesitation?

3. Rekindling the Magic:

Recall a time in childhood when you felt most connected to wonder and mystery.

How can you bring that sense of magic back into your daily life?

Identify one small practice (song, storytelling, time in nature) that can help you reconnect with your inner mystic.

4. Healing Visual Dysbiosis:

Are there areas of your life where you feel trapped by a narrow perspective?

How would your reality shift if you chose to see circumstances as opportunities rather than obstacles?

What practices can help refine your inner vision (meditation, journaling, time in nature)?

5. Returning to Wholeness:

Reflect on a past heartbreak or loss – how has this shaped your evolution?

What attachments are ready to be released in order to step into your sovereignty?

How will you honor your own unfolding and trust that you are exactly where you need to be?

Final Reflection: Write a gratitude statement acknowledging the orchestration in your life. Where do you see divine intelligence at play? How will you choose to trust more fully in the journey ahead?

Mantra for Integration: *I trust the timing, I recognize the signs, I let go of resistance. The universe conspires in my favor.*

The 3rd Realm: Living in Integrity

Integrity: The Law of Circulation

We use our influence, love, touch, and words for three purposes: to bless, to heal, and to prosper. What we send into the world returns to us, for we receive only what we give. Our deeds, thoughts, and words circulate in a cosmic flow, rippling through the unseen and shaping the fabric of our reality.

When we violate the law of love through criticism, resentment, or projection, we set a cycle in motion that inevitably returns to source. Sickness, sorrow, and discord are reflections of the energy we emit. Likewise, acts of kindness, generosity, and truth align us with divine reciprocity, ensuring that what we cultivate within is mirrored in the world around us.

What we wish for another can also be directed back toward us, just as what we say about others may one day be said of us. Even though non-judgment can be challenging when we witness that which does not align with our values, we are better off deflecting energies than absorbing them. We send out only goodwill, without fear. We diffuse what does not carry resonance.

We are incapable of becoming more than what we see ourselves being and limit ourselves to attaining only what we believe we can attain. The mind, like the universe, responds to the frequency we emit. If we hold fast to doubt, scarcity, or limitation, we become the architects of our own obstacles. If we align with faith, trust, and the knowing that we are supported by divine intelligence, we become irresistible magnets for all that belongs to us by sacred design.

As a great teacher once instructed, let us smash and demolish every untrue record in our subconscious mind. Let us rewrite the script with words of power, integrity, and unwavering truth.

Lesson VIII: Embodying Integrity

"Real integrity is doing the right thing, knowing that nobody's going to know whether you did or not." — C.S. Lewis

Integrity is the alignment of thought, word, and action. The embodiment of truth, accountability, and reliability, where what we do and who we are, remain inseparable. The ancients understood that to live without integrity is to live uncentered, disconnected from the self, from nature, and from the divine.

A person who does not walk their talk moves through life fragmented – unembodied, unrooted, and out of sync with their higher purpose. Without integrity, our words become hollow, our promises lose weight, and our presence becomes unstable. Many people feel unfulfilled, restless, and lost because they are not anchored in their purpose.

Integrity is about being honest. This is the foundation of authentic power, the internal compass that keeps us moving in the direction of our highest calling. Confucius taught that integrity is the foundation of virtue, stating: *"The superior man is modest in his speech, but exceeds in his actions."* Integrity is not what we say, but what we do when no one is watching. We embody a willingness to show up fully, to do what is right even when inconvenient, to honor commitments even when difficult.

In Indigenous traditions, integrity is understood as walking in right relationship – with self, with others, and with the Earth. The Lakota people teach *Wolakota*, the principle of harmony through honesty, humility, and action. To break one's word is to disturb the balance not only in one's life, but in the web of existence.

To be whole, we must live in alignment. We walk our talk and honor commitments. In the Bhagavad Gita, Krishna speaks to Arjuna about the duty of action: *"A man who does what he must without attachment to reward, who is firm in his purpose and resolved in his mind – that man is truly noble."* The moment we commit to something – whether a promise, a relationship, or a mission – our integrity is woven into that agreement. To break this accord is not just to fail another, but to weaken our own foundation.

Integrity means being accountable, not seeking perfection. We acknowledge when we fall short, and correct course rather than making excuses. When we lack integrity, we feel this void in our bodies. Our energy is scattered. Our purpose feels blocked. Our relationships suffer. We make commitments we do not keep. We say things we do not mean. We betray our own values and wonder why we feel lost. A person without integrity is like a tree without roots – they may appear strong, but they fall with the first storm.

Integrity does not mean self-sacrifice at the expense of our well-being. Many people betray themselves in the name of pleasing others, saying yes when their spirit says no, compromising to gain approval. The Tao Te Ching teaches: *"Care about what others think, and you will always be their prisoner."* True integrity requires balance – the ability to support others while staying aligned.

When rooted in integrity, our yes is a true yes, and no is a true no. We commit only to what we fully honor. We stand firm in our values, even when tested. We build trust, because others know our word is solid. Integrity is a frequency – a vibration that shapes the reality around us. When we live in integrity, our words create worlds. Our actions build bridges. Our presence becomes medicine, and life begins to flow with effortless alignment.

Walking the Integral Path

Integrity is the weaving of words and action, the alignment of inner knowing with outward expression. To walk in integrity is to be whole, unfractured by doubt, unshaken by external pressures. Integrity is not only a personal vow but a sacred thread that binds us to one another, to the land, to the cosmos.

The path of integrity requires unwavering commitment to truth. The warrior of the heart does not say one thing and do another. When a promise is spoken, this is carried forth with reverence, an offering to the unseen forces that bear witness to all things. Honesty is not merely a virtue but a vibration – one that strengthens the spirit, fortifies relationships, and harmonizes one's place in the great design of existence.

Can you recall a moment of indecision, a time when the desires of the heart conflicted with the perceived obligations of the world? Human struggle often arises from division – between longing and loyalty, between what feels true and what keeps peace. To be integral, one must step away from external expectation and listen to the knowing that whispers from within.

Integrity is the courage to say no when agreement would fracture the self. The discipline to walk away from anything that diminishes authenticity. Integrity is not the act of pleasing others, nor the willingness to compromise truth for convenience. When a path is taken out of fear rather than alignment, a fracture forms – a dissonance that ripples into every aspect of life.

The Hopi teaches that *truth is a living force, not a fixed concept.* To walk in truth is to be in harmony with the flow of creation. This is why the untruthful are never at ease – disharmony creates stagnation, disconnection, and suffering. True peace is found only in alignment.

To embody integrity is to be a beacon – one whom others trust, whose word holds weight. A path of integrity demands accountability:

Honor your word. Speak only what you intend to uphold. Let others trust in your presence, your promise, your follow-through.

Guard your body as a sacred vessel. Nourish yourself with foods that radiate life, move your body with reverence, rest in ways that restore your energy.

Protect your energy. Where you invest time, where you place your currency, what you endorse through your presence – all of these are reflections of your integrity. Be mindful of what you support.

Stand unwavering in truth. Be willing to be misunderstood rather than betray what feels right in your soul.

Integrity is honey in the heart. This is the sweetness that children sense, the grounding presence that allows them to grow without fear. Integrity is tenderness in love, the space held for a partner to unfold without judgment, the unwavering devotion to honoring another with truth rather than illusion.

To walk with integrity does not mean to be without flaw but to meet every misalignment with correction. There is a dance between shadow and light. Shadows arise – patterns of deception, avoidance, or fear. Yet the integral being does not suppress these aspects but brings them to the fire of awareness.

Zen master Reb Anderson teaches that *speech arising from self-concern is false speech.* Buddhism extends honesty beyond transparency – becoming a practice of speech that uplifts, that does not distort for personal gain. The three poisons – greed, hatred, and ignorance – are roots of dishonest expression. Even words of truth, when spoken from malice or superiority, become distorted.

To speak with integrity is to remove oneself from the center of the narrative. If speech seeks validation, control, or advantage, words can become untruthful. Even a half-truth, a carefully curated omission, carries the weight of deception. Before speaking, pause: *What is the intent? Who does this serve?* The integral being speaks not to manipulate but to illuminate.

We want to leave a legacy of integrity. What remains when a life is finished? Titles fade, possessions scatter, but character endures. A life of integrity leaves an imprint – on the hearts touched, wisdom shared, and ways the world was left better than found. The integral path is not about perfection but devotion. This is a daily practice of truth, constant return to alignment, an unwavering commitment to live as one's highest self.

Truth cannot be harmed by untruth. The wind does not struggle to move the mountain, yet in time, the mountain is shaped by the wind. So too does integrity, steady and unyielding, shape the world. Walk this path with reverence, and the universe will conspire to clear the way.

Let each step be a prayer. Let each word be a vow. Let each action reflect truth.

Give What You Need

To walk in integrity is to recognize the reciprocity woven into the fabric of existence. The wind does not hoard the breath of the earth, nor do the rivers withhold their waters from the land. The natural world moves in a rhythm of giving and receiving, an unbroken cycle of nourishment and return. We, too, are bound by this sacred exchange.

The wisdom keepers teach: *We are no greater than the ants and no less than the mountains.* Our reach, our influence, our presence in the world is not determined by status or material accumulation, but by the depth of spirit we carry. The breath of the Creator moves through us in proportion to our willingness to embody her essence.

Two teachings anchor the integral path:

Never take more than you can give.

Give what you need.

These are not mere moral philosophies but vibrational law – principles that govern the unseen forces of balance and harmony.

Giving is an energetic transaction, not solely an exchange of material offerings. To extract energy from another without returning balance is to create disharmony. Lakota natives call this *Wolakota* – a state of peace that arises when all relations exist in balance. When we siphon energy from another without reciprocity, we fracture their sovereignty. To walk in integrity is to ensure that our presence, our words, and our actions contribute to the equilibrium of those around us.

When we receive – whether a gift, a kind word, or an act of generosity – our first thought should not be possession but extension. *Who can I bless in return?* Not as an obligation, but as a natural response to abundance. This is the rhythm of sacred reciprocity, the dance of energy flowing freely rather than being hoarded in fear. Andean peoples speak of *Ayni* – the principle that we are always in relationship, that balance is not static but a continual offering.

When we require something, we give what we need in a different form. If we seek love, we must offer love. If we long for understanding, we must listen deeply to another. If we require support, we must extend our hand to assist someone else. The frequency of giving magnetizes the very thing we seek.

We are invited to align with the flow of creation. Life is not meant to be a series of transactions but a continuous unfolding of generosity. Integrity calls for awareness – of where we hoard, we take without returning, we expect without offering.

To live in alignment with divine orchestration is to recognize that energy moves in spirals, returning always to the source. When we cling, we stagnate. When we release, we receive. The Hopi say: *All that we do to the web of life, we do to ourselves.* Every gesture, every word, every exchange shapes the world we inhabit.

Allow giving to be a prayer and receiving to be a blessing. Let the flow remain unbroken and know that what is given in truth will always find a way back in divine form.

Respect the Work

Talking about possibilities is effortless. Dreaming of abundance, of success, of freedom – all feels within reach when the vision is strong. Yet, the manifestation of greatness does not come from mere longing but from devotion to disciplined effort. The universe responds to action – passivity is not rewarded.

Delusion of entitlement convinces many that life should hand them what they desire without struggle, but those who have achieved true mastery have met the forge of effort with resilience. Unless you are born into inherited wealth, abundance rarely arrives without commitment to the labor that calls in the magic.

Distraction is a great thief of destiny. Tests arise daily – temptations to stray from purpose, invitations to waste time, illusions that seem like opportunity but are merely delay. The wise discern between what is aligned and what is diversion. The integral being does not allow themselves to be pushed and pulled by fleeting distractions but remains centered, dedicated to the work that must be done.

One knows readiness not by external validation, but by the moment distractions lose their grip. When focus sharpens, excuses dissolve, and creation takes precedence over hesitation – this is when the path unfolds. FOMO (fear of missing out) fades in the face of clarity, for what is truly important stands in undeniable priority.

Respect is given to those who stop talking about what they might do and begin the work that transforms vision into reality. The world does not remember those who hesitated, only those who built, who committed, who stepped forward despite uncertainty. Integrity is about truth in action, beyond only words.

The call is clear: Respect the work. Honor the labor. Show up for the vision, and the vision will show up for you.

Wash Yourself of Yourself

"Be melting snow. Wash yourself of yourself. A white flower grows in the quietness. Let your tongue become that flower." – Rumi

The greatest obstacle to evolution is the self – clinging, resisting, and overthinking. Conditioned patterns whisper that control is necessary, worry is productive, and suffering is inevitable, but nature offers another way. Water does not hold onto form; she surrenders to the warmth, dissolving into movement, nourishing all she touches. To be like melting snow is to release all that no longer serves – to let the weight of identity, fear, and limitation dissolve into the current of transformation.

A great teacher instructs, *"When you pay attention to your thoughts and categorize them, they become very powerful. You are feeding them energy because you are not seeing them as simple phenomena. If one tries to quiet them down, that is another way of feeding them."*

Like the snake shedding old skin, integrity calls for renewal. The beliefs, habits, and identities that once protected us can become prisons if held too tightly. The act of washing oneself of oneself is a sacred reciprocity – a return to flow, a release that makes space for new wisdom.

As seasons shift, the glacier releases frozen water, carrying nourishment to distant lands. What was once held is offered freely, returning to the cycle of life. When winter returns, the water freezes again, this time infused with new knowledge, carrying fresh imprints of experience.

To cleanse the self is not to erase identity, but to allow the spirit to expand beyond rigid definitions. In silence, in surrender, in letting go of what has hardened, we attune to a higher frequency. In stillness, the white flower blooms. In release, essence returns. Wash yourself of yourself. Let go and rise anew.

Create the Standard

"The expert in anything was once a beginner."

Who dictates what is perceived as right or wrong? Are there not simply other ways? Lao Tzu believed highly evolved beings rely on conscience as the foundation for pure law. When we root ourselves in the rhythms of the natural world – free from the distortions of media, institutional rhetoric, and prevailing societal poisons – we refine our ability to distinguish good from harmful, truth from deception.

Every framework within culture was once an original thought. Ideologies written into textbooks, timelines crafted into history, and theories accepted as science – all began as seeds of imagination. Someone dared to create. Someone insisted on a new way.

We hold this same power. We are not bound by inherited paradigms. When focus sharpens and distractions dissolve, we have the capacity to override outdated narratives and establish new standards – ones more congruent with the wisdom of the present moment.

This is the invitation:

Question what does not align. Disagree with what is illogical. Trust in your ability to redefine reality. Greatness does not arise from comparison or conformity but from unwavering originality. Your ideas will crystallize. Your truth will illuminate. Your standard will set the course for generations to follow.

Honest Virtues

A wise one omits dishonesty from the culture they proudly represent. Mistruths are not spoken, deception is not entertained, and every word carries the weight of responsibility. While past mistakes may have been marred by corruption, deceit, or self-betrayal, awareness now governs every action. Honesty is a birthright, an inheritance from the divine, not merely a virtue.

Children absorb what they witness, shaping their understanding of truth by observing the integrity – or lack thereof – in those they trust. The honest one understands this, moving with transparency, ensuring every step leaves a legacy of sincerity.

Dishonesty has bruised us all. We have been misled by those we love, deceived by those we trusted, and perhaps most of all, we have betrayed ourselves. Yet, this is a call to action, not a reason to despair. Now is the moment to form alliances of truth, to gather in sacred brotherhood and sisterhood, to forge pacts that ensure our words align with our hearts.

Take time to reflect. What burdens still weigh upon you? What recurring struggles might have been avoided if you had chosen complete honesty? What commitment can you make to embody truthfulness in thought, word, and action?

The Pali Canon teaches *Musavada veramani sikkhapadam samadiyami* – to abstain from falsehood to honor truth as sacred. But truth must be wielded with wisdom. When spoken with malice, even truth becomes a weapon. Sharing a negative experience to tarnish another's reputation, revealing information to gain power over someone – these are dishonest motives wrapped in the guise of honesty. True integrity requires mindfulness. *We vow not to lie but to be truthful.*

Radical responsibility calls for deep self-reflection. Osho's *empty boat* parable teaches this well. When anger arises, the wise do not search for an external cause – they recognize that the storm was already within. The world reflects what we carry inside. Each frustration, every conflict, and all disappointment is a mirror, showing us where growth is needed.

Nothing happens to us; what we experience transpires for us. The lessons we receive are the ones our souls require for evolution. The feedback we encounter, whether painful or affirming, is sacred instruction. Our task is to filter through wisdom, allowing each moment to shape us into beings of deeper integrity.

From the depths of our being, we know this truth: to embody integrity is to walk in love. To be unwavering in virtue is to trust in divine orchestration. To stand fully in honesty is to align with the sacred rhythm of life.

Strength of Man

The potency of a man's strength is demonstrated in his ability to love, capacity to forgive, willingness to compromise, and his unwavering sovereignty in a world conditioned to seek validation from external forces. Strength is not brute force or domination, but gentle resilience that holds steady in the face of adversity.

Pain, loss, and betrayal are not signs of weakness; they are invitations to expand love rather than shrink in fear. When freedom is stripped away, when separation from loved ones feels unbearable, true strength is found in grace to continue loving without hardening the heart. What fuels the spirit to fight for justice, not through rage but through wisdom? What allows one to hold compassion for those who trespass against them? The answer lies in the strength of the heart.

To forgive is not to condone, but to release the weight of bitterness. True strength allows us to see even those who wrong us as wounded children, seeking love just as we have. To hold oneself accountable, to recognize one's own role in conflict, to speak with truth rather than vengeance, this is the way of the sovereign being.

Peace is always superior to confrontation. Calmness overcomes chaos. Love silences hatred. To embody integrity is to rise above reactive impulses and choose a higher path. This is not weakness, but mastery. Saying no to propaganda, rejecting manipulation, and standing in unwavering self-worth are the hallmarks of true sovereignty.

A man who honors the wisdom pulsing through him does not need validation from outside himself. He is whole within himself. He moves with quiet confidence, never diminishing another to elevate himself. Gossip, deceit, and pretense weaken the spirit.

When one attempts to be anything other than their true self, they forfeit their power. True strength is found in radical authenticity, in remaining anchored in truth, in walking with integrity even when the world tries to tempt otherwise. Strength is not in resistance but in fluidity – moving forward with purpose, unshaken by the turbulence of the external world.

To be strong is to be sovereign. To be sovereign is to be free.

Give Them Reasons

"Give the world a reason to remember your name."

Trust is earned through consistency, through the way one moves, speaks, and exists in alignment with truth. To walk in integrity is to give people reasons to trust, to confide, and to recognize authenticity in the rhythm of your actions.

Follow through with your word and assure your people they can count on you. Let your values dictate your movements. Stand unwavering in your truth, knowing that compromise of integrity is a sacrifice too great to bear.

Take care of your health, always. The body is a vessel, a sacred bridge between spirit and earth. Nourish your cells so that you may radiate light wherever you go. Move with presence, allowing your energy to speak before words are even necessary.

Stand for something – never waver for those who attempt to pull you from your course. A rooted tree does not bow to the storm; a sovereign soul does not fold under external pressure. Be mindful of what you support, of where you invest your energy and currency, for these are the seeds that shape the reality around you.

Carry honey in your heart, exude sweetness that leaves an imprint on all who encounter you. Let your children grow up knowing kindness, let your lover feel the sanctuary of your unwavering presence. Hold space, be still when needed, and offer the calmness that soothes the winds of uncertainty.

Honor your commitments, not just to others but to yourself. Accountability is the foundation of integrity – own your missteps, your words, and correct them with grace. Honesty, when rooted in love, becomes a force of clarity, a beacon that calls forth alignment.

Create, always. When we cease to create, we stagnate. Express through music, art, dance, and poetry – through any channel that allows the soul to breathe into form. Time spent in creativity is time spent in expansion.

Gratitude, always. Return, when in scarcity, and in abundance. Acknowledge the sacred nature of every breath, honor the lungs that gift life with each inhale. Move your body, cleanse your energy, and let no stagnation take root in your life.

Dance with your shadows but lead them to light. Release all that diminishes you – whether a job, toxic relationship, poor habits, or limiting beliefs. Absorb wisdom, let go of what no longer serves.

Ego-ficial never outduels the natural. The truest power is not in self-inflation, but in self-awareness.

Remember this: our legacy is not written in accolades or wealth but in character, in the way we made the world better, in the lives we touched, in the love we left behind.

Be Non-Conformist

"Those who know the least obey the best."

True sovereignty cannot be found in conformity. To align with divine integrity is to resist the tides that seek to mold the spirit into something less than designed to be. Healthy femininity and masculinity flourish in non-conformity – standing firm in truth rather than bending to external pressures.

When we allow our well-being and way of life to be dictated by media narratives, propaganda, or societal expectations that do not resonate with our deepest knowing, we relinquish our power. Every day offers an opportunity for reclamation.

Standing for sovereignty means taking our health, our choices, and our spiritual growth into our own hands. We remember that true connection is found in nature, in kinship, in the depths of our own hearts – not in illusions of mainstream distractions.

Maturity is reflected in the ability to hold compassion for those who are bound by fear and manipulation. To remain humble is to recognize that we are not above or below anyone, but walking side by side, shaping the world through our actions. Grace flows effortlessly when the heart is pure, the mind is clear, and when fear has been released.

Refuse to conform to what does not serve truth. Trust in the flow of divine alignment, not the intercepted currents of coercion. Walk with integrity, speak with clarity, and let your very being, be a testament to the power of sovereignty.

The Grace of Humility

Growing up around those who are emotionally underdeveloped and psychologically immature can stunt growth. Maturity arrives when we no longer feel compelled to associate with or idolize individuals who are not moving steadily toward a higher purpose. The more we listen to our guiding forces and trust in the direction they lead us, the clearer our vision becomes.

Before we satisfy the demands of instant gratification, we must honor three pivotal components of expansion: identifying purpose, recognizing what drives us, and safeguarding our health and well-being. An embodied being is a mature being.

Growth requires the acquisition of wisdom and knowledge. As we learn, we remember. Each experience, every encounter, becomes ingrained in the lessons we embody. We reflect on our wrongs – they teach us new songs. We make peace with our losses, forgive betrayals, and reconcile with love. We release old stories that no longer define us.

Maturity is reflected in our ability to hold compassion for those who are bound to lower frequencies, to speak kindly of others or say nothing at all, and to discern when silence holds greater power than words spoken from bitterness. To be humble is to know we are neither above nor below anyone. We stand side by side, face to face, back-to-back. How we carry ourselves, how we hold our composure, nourish our body, mind, and spirit – all of this is displayed in our health, our presence, and the light we radiate.

Grace exudes from within when the heart is pure, when shadows are no longer feared but transformed, and when fear is surrendered in the presence of truth.

The Fortitude of Morale

True morale is the embodiment of resilience, the unwavering commitment to truth and purpose, not blind optimism or avoidance of struggle. As we ascend in character, our energy levels follow. Muscles strengthen, not only in form but in discipline. Our values sharpen, and our presence becomes a beacon of integrity.

Command and conquer as we have known has expired. The world no longer needs leaders who take by force but those who stand in unwavering conviction. We do not conquer others, we transcend ourselves. We take command of our lives through accountability, mindful action, and the daily discipline of honoring what is sacred.

The Bhagavad Gita speaks of the warrior Arjuna, frozen in battle, questioning whether he should fight. Lord Krishna teaches him: *A person is only entitled to the work, never to the bore fruit. Let not the results of action be your motive, nor be attached to inaction.* This is the lesson of morale – acting not for outcome, but because integrity demands we do.

Consider the endurance of the Buddha, who sat beneath the Bodhi tree, unwavering in his pursuit of enlightenment, even as Mara – the demon of doubt – tempted him with illusions. He did not waver, for his resolve was built not on fleeting motivation but on an unshakable foundation of truth.

Morale is our spiritual stamina. The wisdom to hold faith in divine timing, to persist through trials without losing heart. Like the samurai who meditates before the sword is drawn, like the monk who sweeps the temple floor as an act of devotion, like the elder who plants a tree knowing he will never sit in her shade – we act with integrity not for recognition, but because of who we are.

In moments of fatigue, doubt, or uncertainty, we remember: The storm does not last forever, and the river never stops flowing. Integrity is the river – steadfast, unyielding, and always returning to source.

May our strength be in our honor. Allow our morale to be unwavering. Let our actions be a testament to the sacred path we walk.

Key Takeaways from Lesson VIII

Integrity as Alignment

Integrity is the harmony between thought, word, and action.

When we live in alignment, we cultivate fulfillment, trust, and purpose.

Indigenous wisdom teaches us that integrity is about walking in right relationship – with ourselves, others, and the Earth.

Walking the Integral Path

Integrity demands truth, consistency, and accountability.

To be integral, one must step away from external validation and listen to the deep knowing within.

The Hopi teach that truth is a living force – not fixed but fluid, adapting yet unwavering.

Sacred Reciprocity: Give What You Need

The universe mirrors our actions – what we give we receive.

The Lakota principle of *Wolakota* teaches that balance and harmony arise when we honor energetic exchanges.

True wealth comes from circulation, not accumulation.

Respect the Work

Integrity means honoring commitments, focusing on purpose, and resisting distractions.

Success is earned through consistency and devotion.

The Strength of True Sovereignty

Power is not found in force, but in unwavering self-ownership.

Strength is demonstrated through love, forgiveness, and the ability to remain centered in chaos.

Integrity calls for discernment – knowing when to stand firm and when to release what no longer serves.

Honest Virtues: Truth as a Way of Life

Honesty is not just about words, but the purity of intention behind them.

Zen wisdom reminds us that even truth can be a weapon if wielded with malice.

The Pali Canon teaches *Musavada veramani sikkhapadam samadiyami* – a vow to abstain from falsehood and honor the sacred power of speech.

Becoming the Standard

All structures, belief systems, and paradigms were once ideas – integrity allows us to shape new realities.

Non-conformity is necessary when the world moves out of alignment with truth.

When we embody integrity, we naturally influence those around us to rise.

The Grace of Humility

True maturity is reflected in our ability to hold compassion, release ego, and move with grace.

Humility is not self-diminishment – this is standing in truth without arrogance.

The Tao Te Ching teaches, *"Care about what others think, and you will always be their prisoner."*

The Fortitude of Morale

Strength comes from unwavering faith in one's path.

The Bhagavad Gita reminds us that true warriors act without attachment to outcomes.

Integrity builds resilience, allowing us to persist without wavering, even in uncertainty.

Reflect & Apply Worksheet

1. Personal Integrity Assessment

In what areas of your life do you feel most aligned with integrity?

Where do you feel out of alignment? What shifts can you make?

When have you compromised your truth to please others? How did this feel?

2. The Power of Your Word

Think of a promise you made but did not keep – how did that impact trust in yourself or others?

What commitments do you currently hold? Are there any you need to adjust to honor them fully?

Write a declaration of integrity – what values will you stand by no matter the challenge?

3. Reciprocity in Action

What is something you deeply desire? How can you give that to others?

How can you practice *Ayni* (sacred reciprocity) in your relationships?

Reflect on a time you received an unexpected blessing. What did you give that allowed this to come to you?

4. Mastering Focus & Discipline

Identify your biggest distractions – how do they pull you from integrity?

What is one discipline you can commit to daily that will strengthen your alignment?

How do you define success beyond external validation?

5. Sovereignty & Strength

Where in your life do you feel most sovereign? Where do you still seek validation?

How do you respond to conflict? Do you remain in integrity even when tested?

Write a forgiveness letter – to yourself or someone else – to release burdens and restore energy.

6. Honesty & Communication

Are there any half-truths or omissions you have spoken that weigh on you?

How do you ensure your words uplift rather than manipulate?

Commit to one practice of radical honesty this week.

7. Redefining Leadership

What beliefs or societal norms have you conformed to that do not serve your highest path?

What does this mean to you to *"become the standard"*?

Write a vision statement for the impact you wish to make.

8. Embodying Humility & Strength

How do you balance humility with confidence?

What practices keep you grounded when facing success or recognition?

Who do you admire for their integrity? What lessons can you take from them?

9. Resilience & Morale

How do you stay committed when results are not immediate?

What spiritual or personal disciplines strengthen your morale?

What is one mantra or affirmation that reminds you to stay steadfast?

Final Reflection: Write a statement of gratitude for the ways integrity has shaped your life. How has walking in truth led to alignment and fulfillment?

Mantra for Integration: *I stand in truth. I honor my words. I walk in integrity, unwavering and whole.*

Lesson IX: Showing Your Children a Good Way

"Children learn more from what you are than what you teach."
— W.E.B. Du Bois

Our children do not inherit only our words, they are entrusted with our actions, energy, habits, and our way of being. To raise a child in truth, purity, and wisdom is not to fill their mind with knowledge, but to nourish their soul with presence. The ancients understood that children do not need to be taught as much as they need to be shown.

We are required to prioritize our role in conscious parenting. In Indigenous traditions, parenting is considered a sacred trust, a duty that extends beyond the present moment and reaches seven generations into the future. Lakota people speak of the *"Mitákuye Oyás'iŋ"* – the understanding that all things are interconnected, and the ways in which we guide our children ripples outward, shaping the balance of life.

Hopi elders remind us: *"We are the ones we have been waiting for."* We are the ancestors our children will one day call upon. We are the living prayers of those who came before us. How we walk today determines the world they will inherit.

To be a conscious parent is to cultivate an environment where a child thrives in wisdom, purity, and clarity, not in confusion, distortion, and artificial influences. We must teach through example rather than words.

Confucius taught: *"To put the world in order, we must first put the nation in order; to put the nation in order, we must first put the family in order; to put the family in order, we must first cultivate our personal life; to cultivate our personal life, we must first set our hearts right."* If we wish to raise children who are honest, wise, and kind, we must first embody these virtues ourselves.

If we tell them to be patient, yet react in anger, if we tell them to be present, yet escape into distractions, if we tell them to live purely, yet indulge in vices, they will see the truth beneath our words.

Children mirror energy, not empty instruction. This is why the great Zen masters taught through action, silence, and stillness. A child learns mindfulness not from being told to meditate, but from watching a parent move with grace, patience, and attentiveness. The choices we make today do not end with us. They weave into the fabric of our lineage, either breaking cycles of suffering or reinforcing them. Our goal is to break lineal trauma and experience the healing required for seven generations.

Modern science affirms what ancient wisdom has always known – trauma, addiction, fear, and emotional wounds are passed down epigenetically, imprinted in our DNA. When violence, neglect, or dishonesty exist in a lineage, an awakened soul is empowered to break the pattern. This is our task. To cleanse our line of:

Fear that teaches survival over joy.

Anger that turns into shame.

Habits that deplete, rather than replenish.

We do not heal for ourselves alone. We heal for our children, our grandchildren, and the generations we will never meet. In the words of Iroquois wisdom keepers: *"In our every deliberation, we must consider the impact of our decisions on the next seven generations."*

When we are healed, our presence encourages inner peace, strength, and purity in children. A child raised with presence, patience, and clarity will not need to unlearn confusion and suffering later in life. A child taught to honor the elements, the forests, the rivers, the stars, will never be lost in a world of artificial light. A child raised in love and sovereignty will never feel the need to seek validation in external distractions.

We must teach them to:

Trust their intuition over societal expectations.

Find strength in stillness, rather than chaos.

Revere nature as their greatest teacher.

Nourish their bodies with what fuels life, not what depletes.

To show children a good way is the path forward and requires that we first walk this way ourselves. We are to be the example, the steady presence, the unshaken guide. We are instructed with divine guidance to build a world where they never have to recover from their childhoods, where they grow in an environment that fosters clarity, wonder, and sovereignty. If we do this, we will not need to correct them later. They will already know the way.

My approach to parenting is simple: *How can I be the person for my children that I always needed throughout my life?* The one they feel safe with, who listens without judgment, who they know is always there to share wisdom, to guide them, and to love them unconditionally. The one who leads by example, embodying health, integrity, and authenticity. How do I show up in ways that imprint on them a deep knowing of their worth, a sense of curiosity for the world, and an unshakable foundation of goodness?

I vow to always be a source of calmness for my children when chaos ensues around them. If I remain centered, they are less likely to be swayed by the storms of the world. There is no reason for me to raise my voice, to command through fear – because true respect is not demanded but earned. When I move with patience, when I uphold gentleness within my strength, they absorb this same peace. They learn discernment not through rigid instruction but through the quiet guidance of example.

Another pledge of mine is to be patient with them. Rushed energy creates tension, and tension leads to disharmony. I commit to being present, to listening deeply, to ensuring they always know they are seen, heard, and valued.

I often wonder how different my life would have been had I known, as a child, that there was another way to live – if someone had guided me toward a path of nourishment, consciousness, and truth. What if I had never been stuck in places I did not belong, surrounded by those consuming the same poisons I once did? What if I had always known how to honor my body as sacred?

The guiding forces in my life tell me the answer: *Be that person for others.* Help make life easier for those who come after. Show up in ways I once wished others had shown up for me. This is not just the task of a parent, but of all who walk this path.

We do this for our children, for the ones we love, and for every soul we encounter. We live with integrity, we lead with love, and we embody the wisdom we wish we had been given.

Move Slow

A great lesson in parenting, as the years pass swiftly, is to move slowly. When we slow our breathing, quiet our thoughts, and embrace the fullness of each moment, we expand the time we share. The rushing world teaches urgency, but the wisdom keepers know better – life is best lived in presence, not in haste.

Lao Tzu reminds us: *"Nature does not hurry, yet everything is accomplished."* The river does not force a way to the ocean, the tree does not strain to bear fruit before season. Likewise, our children grow not by force, but by nurture – by the steady rhythm of a home filled with patience, love, and the space to bloom in their own time.

Remember *Wolakota* – living in peace and balance with all things. To move slowly is to live in right relationship with time, to understand that presence is the true currency of love. A hurried life teaches children that what matters most is what is next. A slow, mindful life teaches them that what matters most is what is now.

Our prayer is that our children's exuberance remains uncorrupted, that they always remember to use their voice and stand firm in their center. May their emotionality stay uninhibited, their natural ways unrestrained. May they never be tamed by the fears of rejection, by rigid rules that suppress their essence, or by routines incongruent with their soul's mission.

The Hopi say: *"Take nothing lightly. Hold everything sacred."* When we move slowly, we honor the sacredness of every moment. We model for our children a life where nothing is rushed but everything is received in divine timing. They learn by our example that presence is protection, patience is strength, and that time is a gift meant to be savored, not squandered.

Our invocation is for them to always be protected, safe, and healthy. To know that life is not a race but a dance, a prayer, a sacred unfolding. When we slow down, we do not lose time – we expand the universe around us. In this expansion, we create a space where childhood is not rushed away, but treasured, where wisdom is not spoken in haste, but embodied in stillness. We walk with them, showing them the way, one unhurried step at a time.

Revering Precious Moments in Parenting

Parenting in alignment with integrity and love requires deep reverence for the fleeting moments of childhood. The days may seem long, but the years pass swiftly. When we are fully present, we extend time, creating a life where each sacred moment is not overlooked but honored.

A child's need for connection is often expressed in the simplest ways – requests to be held, to be fed, to be tucked in at night. These are not burdens, but invitations. Invitations to step into stillness, to embrace the magic of the now, to witness the world through their eyes before they grow beyond the need to ask.

I cherish the moments when my son asks me to hold him, especially at night when he wants to step outside and gaze at the sky. Standing beneath the Milky Way, pointing to constellations, marveling at the holes to heaven, we whisper wishes on shooting stars – to always have more moments like this, to always be close.

Indigenous teachings remind us that our children are not truly ours; they belong to the universe, to the Earth, to the stars they gaze upon. The Hawaiian 'ohana concept teaches that family is a sacred bond woven into the very fabric of existence. To parent consciously is to honor this sacred trust, ensuring our children feel deeply seen, deeply loved, and forever connected to something greater.

Children thrive when they know they are safe. Not only physically, but emotionally, energetically. The wind blows through the coconut palms, and my son startles at the sound of rustling leaves. I assure him this is only the elements dancing, the Earth breathing alongside us. In my arms, he feels secure.

The great Zen masters taught through action, not words. They understood that a child will not remember every lesson spoken, but they will always carry the energy of what was demonstrated. When I remain patient, when I move with grace, when I embrace stillness in his presence, I teach him peace without speaking a word.

One day, he will no longer ask to be carried. So even when my arms grow tired, I hold him as long as he needs. Because time will shape him into a man who no longer reaches for me, but will always remember that when he did, I was there. As he grows, these moments will transform.

One day, he will make meals with me instead of asking me to be fed. I will follow behind him as he climbs mountains, guiding him only when necessary. He will stand atop Haleakalā and direct the prayers. He will swim farther than me, laughing at the waves that once made him hesitate. He will compose his own poetry, his own songs, perhaps playing the guitar better than I ever could. Together, we will still sing beneath the moon's glow.

The wisdom of our children will one day surpass our own, and when this time arrives, I will listen intently, absorbing his insights, exchanging stories across generations. The trees bend to witness a love like this. The flowers bloom in quiet reverence. A love so vast, even the trillions of microorganisms that sustain life pause in honor. This is the bond between parent and child. A universal frequency that carries through time, never fading, always returning. A love that is sacred, unwavering, and everlasting.

A Child's Requirements

A child does not ask for perfection. A child asks for presence. When my son looked into my eyes and said, *"You're the only Dad I would have ever picked,"* I felt an immediate wave of emotion – gratitude, reverence, and an unshakable responsibility to honor this sacred trust. His sincerity awakened something deep within me – a warrior, not of battle, but of devotion. A father who will always fight for more time, more moments, more love.

Children require connection, not distractions. They require our full attention, undivided presence, and willingness to step outside the constellations of our busyness and see them – truly see them. A child thrives when we slow down, when we sit with them, create with them, laugh with them, and listen to them, and at the same depth we wish to be heard. Whether we are playing music together in the stillness of an arctic night or preparing meals in a quiet home, *being there* is more important than grand gestures.

For children of separated families, the time apart can be a weight on the heart. As a single father, I know the ache of limited time, the heaviness of parting ways after brief visits, and the silent prayers that one day, the distance will lessen. But within that time apart, I trust that our bond remains unbreakable. That when we reunite, we pick up right where we left off – without hesitation, without loss, only love.

The way knows how to guide us in parenting. When uncertainty arises, or we feel the pull to react rather than respond, we pause. We breathe. We ask for divine guidance in how to proceed. A child's requirements are simple: love, presence, and the knowing that we will always be there. Not just in body, but in spirit, devotion, and a steadfast frequency of love that never wavers.

Dad's Matter

A father's presence is a child's birthright, not just a privilege. Fatherhood is a sacred role, woven into the fabric of a child's sense of self-worth, strength, and stability. A father's absence leaves an imprint; a father's devotion shapes a legacy.

We finished making juice, and I started strumming the guitar, singing to my son. The last night of this visit. He got teary-eyed and asked, *"Dad, what am I going to do without you?"* My chest felt hollow. What was I going to do without him? How do I answer when I know I cannot provide the comfort he seeks in my response? I wrapped him up in my arms and cried with him. *"You're going to continue to shine, Arlo."*

A father's role in a child's life is irreplaceable. No system, no court, no external force should ever be allowed to sever the sacred bond between father and child. The wisdom keepers of old knew this well. In Lakota tradition, fathers were integral to a child's education, guiding them through rites of passage, teaching them the ways of the land, and modeling strength through wisdom rather than force.

In Hawaiian culture, the *makua kāne* – the father – was seen as a pillar of protection, discipline, and guidance, instilling in his children a deep respect for their ancestors, their land, and their purpose. Removing a father from his child's life was seen as an act that disrupted not just the family, but the harmony of the universe.

A father's rights are not about him – they are about the child's inherent right to grow up with the presence, guidance, and love of their dad. To take a father away is to take away a child's sense of security, to create a void where wholeness should exist.

I spent years as a volunteer for Big Brothers, Big Sisters, knowing firsthand the impact a childhood without a father has on self-esteem, character, and worth. I showed up for children who had no father figure because I understood what was at stake. Now, as a father myself, I am forced to navigate a system that treats fatherhood as conditional, as if my presence is optional rather than essential. I know the weight of parting ways after a visit, the ache of watching my son and daughter grow through a screen, the quiet prayers that the distance will one day be shortened.

The prisons of the world are filled with fatherless sons. The streets are lined with children who never knew the embrace of a dad who told them they mattered. A child without a father does not just lose a parent; they lose a guidepost, a protector, a mirror of their own worth.

When I was growing up, I never needed the world to affirm my values. I knew them, because I had a father who showed up. Who told me I was important. Who made me feel that I was enough. My son deserves the same. All children do.

Fathers matter. Our presence is a necessity, not a privilege. No agenda, no law, no societal structure should have the power to rewrite that truth.

The way forward is clear:

We must fight for our place in our children's lives, not through conflict, but through unwavering commitment.

We must remind the world that a father's love is not secondary, but foundational.

We must refuse to let our children grow up wondering why they were kept from us, questioning their worth.

Fatherhood is sacred. Now is the time that the world remembers this truth.

Sweet Child: A Message for the Next Generation

"You are made of Earth, sweet child. Here to play in the warmth of the sun, bare feet in the dirt, running wild. You were born to make a difference, to be someone."

Children are born with an inherent magic – an untamed spirit, an unfiltered love, an unshakable belief in the goodness of life. Their laughter heals wounds unseen, their innocence reminds us of what the world was meant to be. They arrive with wonder in their eyes, not yet conditioned by limitations, not yet dulled by the expectations of society.

In many Indigenous cultures, children are seen as sacred beings – closer to the divine than adults, carrying wisdom from the realms before birth. Lakota natives believe that children come into the world with a deep knowing, and our role as parents and elders is to nourish this knowing, not to impose.

We must remind them:

That their curiosity is their compass, leading them toward discovery, growth, and joy.

That their kindness is a strength, not a weakness.

That the world will try to shape them into something smaller than they are, but they were born to take up space, to shine, to be free.

A child raised in love becomes a beacon of light. A child raised in restriction learns only fear. Our task is to protect their purity – not by shielding them from the world, but by giving them the tools to walk with grace, strength, and an unwavering sense of self.

"You are made from elements, enriched with ancient light and cosmic elegance. Here to dance beneath the stars. You were born to help us remember who we are."

There is no force greater than a child's love. Love from children disarms anger, softens the hardest of hearts. Their hands, small but mighty, carry prayers into the world. Their voices, full of wonder, remind us to look up, to dream, to believe in things that are shrouded. We must teach them to honor their emotions, to trust their intuition, to be fearless in their kindness. The world will try to harden them – but we must show them another way.

"You are made of love, sweet child. Your heart lifts hatred up out of this matrix and invites a loving embrace. You were born to remind us that our purpose is not to chase or always search for ways to win some race that leads to a non-existent place."

Our children are the keepers of a new world. One that is not built on division, but unity. Not on conquest, but cooperation. Not on fear, but love. We must nurture this world within them, so that when they step forward to lead, they do so with the courage to be kind, the strength to be gentle, and the wisdom to remain true to who they are.

"You are made for this Earth, sweet child. You are free to think your own thoughts. Your presence is all that is required."

Let them grow wild. Let them be whole. Let them teach us what we have forgotten. Above all, let us never forget to tell them how deeply, how endlessly, they are loved.

Ode to Mothers: Honoring the Givers of Life

Mothers are the embodiment of creation, the vessels through which life enters this world, the nurturers who sacrifice endlessly for the well-being of their children. Their devotion is woven into the fabric of existence, and their presence forms the foundation of every soul they raise.

A mother offers her body, her comfort, her energy, her years – all in service to the sacred task of creation and care. She labors through delivery, endures nights without sleep, and spends the days of her children's youth ensuring their needs are met before her own. Then, after years of holding, teaching, guiding, and loving, she must face the grief of letting go.

In many Indigenous cultures, motherhood is revered as the highest role in the sacred circle of life. The Navajo people honor *Shimá*, the mother, as the first teacher and protector, the one who weaves harmony into the home. In Andean traditions, Pachamama – the great Earth Mother – is seen as the ultimate provider, always giving, always nourishing, even when unrecognized.

To devote so much, knowing that one day a child will walk their own path, start their own family, and no longer need the daily presence of their mother, this is the quiet sacrifice of motherhood. A lasting act of unconditional love, a giving without expectation.

My mother never gave up on me, even when I was not on the best path in my younger years. She taught me to bloom where I am planted, just as the flowers do, and because of this, everywhere I go, I shine. To honor our mothers is to acknowledge the depth of their sacrifice and the boundlessness of their love. We give thanks, not just in words, but in how we carry their lessons forward.

We must show them appreciation while they are here, not only in their absence. We recognize that their guidance shaped us, even in ways we did not understand at the time. We give back in love and presence, ensuring they never feel forgotten.

The cycle of motherhood is the cycle of nature – nurturing, letting go, and watching from a distance as the seeds planted grow into their own.

To every mother, past and present, we honor you. For the love you have given, for the strength you have carried, for the sacrifices unseen. You are the givers of life, the first homes we ever knew, and the reason we continue to grow.

Great Teachers: Embodying the Lessons We Share

Great teachers are not just those who speak wisdom, they are those who live with this embodiment. Their actions align with their words, their integrity remains unwavering, and their presence becomes a lesson.

The Hopi believes that true wisdom is not taught but demonstrated. In Indigenous traditions, elders do not instruct through commands, but through the example of their daily lives. The way they walk, the way they listen, the way they move with reverence, this is the teaching.

Great teachers are disciplined in their craft.

Their quality of life is a testament to their principles.

They are devoted students of irrefutable mastery.

To be a teacher is to be a guide, a torchbearer illuminating the path of truth. Find refuge in learning under divine guidance. Let your connection to infinite source expand. Find God while searching for yourself.

On your quest to come back to your center, acknowledge that the divine guides who protect and support you on your mission have placed their trust in you to be an authentic, clear, and radiant force for assisting others in finding their way to purity.

Be dedicated and loyal to this life path. Make the declaration that you will not bend or break. This assures we do not betray the angels who are instructing us and feeding us the knowledge and wisdom required to fulfill our life's work.

The Cosmic Dandelion: Planting Seeds of Goodness

Children, when raised in love, truth, and alignment, become cosmic dandelions – carrying seeds of wisdom and light that take root wherever they go. Their presence is not just a reflection of our teachings, but a testament to the care, patience, and integrity with which they were nurtured.

Lakota people believe that children are sacred beings, sent from the spirit world to remind us of our purpose. They are not possessions, but entrusted souls who will one day plant their own roots, shaping the world through the lessons we have imparted.

A child raised in sovereignty will walk in truth. A child raised in reverence will respect all life. A child raised in clarity will not be swayed by the illusions of the world. Like dandelion seeds, their presence will drift far beyond our sight, but their impact will remain – woven into the fabric of a changing planet.

My son, Arlo, embodies this truth. He carries light in his laughter, wisdom in his wonder, and strength in his gentleness. I wrote this for him, knowing that one day, he will scatter his own seeds of goodness across the earth:

Your might is derived from your heart. There is magic in the way you bring delight to so many lives. The elegance of your vibe.

There is ferocity in your gentleness. The strength you embody emanates in your innocence. You are as bright as you are powerful.

Your mind will always outduel those who command, colonize, and take what they mine. Your wisdom is the ancient, primordial kind.

Through tenderness you will find ways to attract what helps you shine. Divinity has a color the same as your eyes.

You smile and portals open to Zion.

A cosmic dandelion.

Leaving permanent traces of your exuberance wherever you fly.

To raise a child in a good way is not to mold them into something of our making, but to give them the tools to remain whole. We show them by example what integrity looks like, what love feels like, and what strength truly is. When we do this, they will not only flourish, but they will carry the essence of what they have learned into every corner of existence.

Like the dandelion, they will spread beauty, healing, and wisdom wherever the wind takes them. In their journey, they will remind the world that purity, once planted, never fades.

The Art & Power of Play: Keeping the Spirit of Wonder Alive

Play is a constant necessity, not a pastime. The purest form of expression, a direct channel to creativity, curiosity, and joy. When we remove play from our lives as adults, we do more than lose a source of enjoyment – we suppress our spirit.

Animals do not play because they are young; they remain young because they play. Wolves chase each other in open fields, birds dance in the air, dolphins surf the waves. Play is connection, renewal, and survival, not wasted energy.

A child's world is built on play. This represents how they explore, test boundaries, and make sense of life. Indigenous cultures honor this truth. In many Native traditions, children are given the freedom to run, climb, dig, and immerse themselves in the natural world, understanding that these moments of joy shape their resilience, intelligence, and well-being.

When we do not have access to a piece of earth to dig in, we lose our connection to the land. If there are no trees to climb, we require stimulation from artificial sources. When there is no fresh fruit to gather, we resort to consuming what is placed before us, often processed and lifeless.

If wild animals no longer roam free, we forget the importance of protecting them. Without fertile soil for planting seeds, we lose gratitude for the food that sustains us. When clean water vanishes, we lose our instinct to leap, dive into, and feel the sacred embrace of freshwater.

All mammals establish a sense of play as they discover, evolve, and mature. Our play circuits are always present, waiting to be reawakened. Neural circuits associated with our sense of play can be switched back on at any stage of life. As we integrate play into our lives, neurological activity increases, and the chemistry of our brain changes, enhancing our ability to feel joy, adapt, and create.

To deprive children of nature is to deprive them of what constitutes life. To replace authentic play with artificial entertainment is to dull their senses, weaken their spirit, and disconnect them from their primal wisdom. An ideal path to the development and regulation of a healthy nervous system is through time spent outdoors, through movement, through play. Running, climbing, jumping, and splashing are not mere activities. They are ceremonies of connection and rituals of vitality.

The Hopi believe that a child raised in nature grows into a balanced adult, one who respects the land, their own body, and the harmony of existence. The Lakota says that a child allowed to play freely carries the wisdom of the ancestors in their bones.

This is an invitation to reacquaint ourselves with the art of play. To nurture the spirit of joy within us. To let our children teach us what we have forgotten – that laughter is medicine, that movement is life, that to truly live is to never stop playing.

Climb a tree.

Dig your hands into the soil.

Swim in waters untamed.

Chase the wind.

Dance with no reason other than the joy of motion.

Let us raise children who never lose their sense of wonder as we reclaim this remembrance within ourselves. For the spirit that plays is the spirit that thrives.

Lions Gate Love: Honoring a Child's Milestones

A child's journey through life is filled with transitions, moments of growth that bring both excitement and uncertainty. Each passing year, each birthday, marks an evolution – one that should be met with reverence, patience, and gentle encouragement.

On the eve of my son's sixth birthday, he turned to me and said, *"Dad, I am scared to turn six because I have never been six before."* His words carried an innocence, a purity, that resonated deeply. I remembered the child within me who also faced the unknown with similar hesitation.

I told him to allow his feelings to be present, to honor them, and that when he woke up, he would be six, and not much would have changed. When the morning came, I asked, *"Arlo, you are six now. Did anything change?"* He grinned and dramatically replied, *"Oh no, Dad, look! My thumb got bigger. I'm scared!"*

This moment, even being so lighthearted, held a sacred truth – growth is constant, and each stage of life is a threshold we must cross with grace. Just as children transition into new phases, so too must parents. Our role is to create a space where they feel safe to evolve, where they are met with reassurance rather than fear, guidance rather than pressure.

Every milestone, every rite of passage, is an opportunity to affirm their strength, their resilience, and their readiness to embrace life's unfolding path. Through their journey, we too are reminded to embrace our own evolution – to meet change with wonder rather than resistance, with joy rather than fear.

For our children, we hold space. For ourselves, we learn to trust. In doing so, we show them a way that is not burdened by worry but illuminated by love.

Protect What You Love

When a child smiles, the world shifts. Their joy radiates in ways that transform the spaces around them, warming everything they touch. When we are fully present with our children, we understand that our greatest responsibility is to protect this light – to ensure they grow in an environment where they feel safe, seen, and free to thrive.

The best way to love our children is to keep ourselves whole. If a child sees a parent unhappy, they will feel something is wrong. If we are unhealthy, if we abuse our bodies, if we exist in constant stress, they will absorb these patterns as their own. If we live in balance, with vitality and clarity, they will mirror this state of being.

Children are great imitators. They pick up not only our words but our posture, habits, reactions. If we rush through life without presence, they learn urgency. If we respond with impatience, they learn frustration. When we move with grace and navigate the world with love and mindfulness, they absorb this as well.

This is an invitation to be patient with our children. To be conscious of what we model for them.

Never project anger onto them.

Let them know they are safe in your presence.

Be the calm they can always depend on.

Show them joy, show them kindness, show them how to honor their bodies with clean air, water, and nourishment.

Read to them often.

Speak words of encouragement.

To protect what we love is to honor the sacred role of parenthood. We embody the presence we wish for them to carry forward, ensuring that in their hearts, they will always know they are enough.

The Vastness of Pretty: Holding Reverence for Our Children

Children are the embodiment of our lineage, the living continuation of our prayers, dreams, and sacrifices. To look upon them with reverence is to honor the generations before and after us, to see the vastness of creation reflected in their being.

Choctaw people teach that children are sacred, a gift from Hashtali, the Great Spirit. They arrive carrying wisdom from the obscured world, unburdened by the limitations imposed by society. Many Indigenous cultures believe that children choose their parents before birth, selecting the ones who will guide them through this life. To be entrusted with a child is to receive a profound responsibility – to nurture them in love, to teach them with kindness, and to see them not as possessions, but as divine beings unfolding into their purpose.

My daughter, Nevaeh, in all her radiance, reminds me daily of the sacredness of this task. She is the light of my lineage, a bridge between past and future. I wrote this in honor of her, a reminder of the infinite beauty she carries:

Lineages of trauma vanish to her beauty.

Oceans could never be as vast as she is pretty.

Haiku jungles are not as lush as her presence is enough.

Gratitude fills me up.

To receive the honor of learning from my daughter.

How to remain calm, emanate gentle strength, help her feel safe.

Picking Jamaican lilikoi from trees to enjoy their sweetness together.

I am thankful forever.

To hold reverence for a child is to hold reverence for life. They remind us of the purity we once carried, the wonder we must protect, the kindness we must embody. The way we treat them shapes not only their reality but the world they will one day create.

We must teach our children:

That their presence is enough.

That they are loved beyond words.

That their voice matters.

That they are the continuation of something far greater than themselves.

To love a child in a good way is to witness their vastness, to honor the sacredness of their existence, to nurture their spirit with patience, and to ensure that in their presence, the world feels just a little bit brighter.

See God in Others: Honoring the Divine in Every Child

A child is the embodiment of divinity, a living expression of creation's most sacred force. To see God in a child is to recognize the purity, wisdom, and infinite light they carry. In many Indigenous traditions, children are believed to be closest to the spirit world, untouched by the limitations of the material realm. They arrive in this world as divine messengers, bringing with them clarity that we, as adults, must protect and honor.

The Maya speaks of *k'uxaaj*, the sacred heart, a knowing that resides in every child. Our duty as parents and elders is to nurture this heart, to ensure she remains open, unburdened by fear, and full of love. The role of a parent is not to shape a child into something else, but to guide them as they unfold into their true essence.

We must learn to see children not as blank slates to be written upon, but as sacred vessels carrying the divine. When we honor the God within them, we shape a world where children feel loved, respected, and empowered to walk with reverence and pride.

This is our responsibility – to ensure they grow up knowing they are whole, they are powerful, and they are never alone. To see the divine in a child is to see the divine in ourselves, in the world, in all things. When we do this, we walk in reverence, we teach through love, and we create a lineage of light that will endure for generations to come.

I wrote this for my children, Arlo and Nevaeh, as a reminder that in their eyes, I see the face of God:

I see God as I witness you.

Being your Dad, my gratitude accrues.

The moments I questioned my faith turn to ash, and I detach from holding any of my love back.

When she found you, Starlight knew she met her match.

Beautiful crashed into an oceanic maze and spread your elements across the waves of what have now formed into the potency of who you are.

The full moon glow that beams through your eyes. Never have I gazed into more divine streams of blue. There is endless diversity in your hues.

To be the best I can, to always assure you are protected, for you to know who I am, these are the most important goals I pursue.

As parents, we hold the duty to not bring our confusion into a child's sphere. To honor the clarity in their innocence. We allow them to seek out their vision clear, without projecting our desires, wants, or fears.

I see spirit showing you the way. Enriching your identity. Glowing in your grace.

I am here to support you as you age. For you to feel safe so you can accomplish what you were brought into this life to create.

No person could ever take this away.

Key Takeaways from Lesson IX

Conscious Parenting as a Sacred Trust

Children do not inherit just our words; they absorb our actions, energy, and presence.

Indigenous traditions emphasize raising children with the awareness that their growth ripples across seven generations.

Confucius reminds us that to raise children in truth, we must first cultivate integrity within ourselves.

Move Slow: The Power of Presence

Slowing down creates deeper connection and presence with our children.

The Hopi teach, *"Take nothing lightly. Hold everything sacred."* Every moment is an opportunity to instill peace and security.

A hurried life teaches children urgency and anxiety, while a mindful life teaches patience and contentment.

Revering Precious Moments in Parenting

Each moment with a child is a sacred gift; presence matters more than grand gestures.

Zen masters taught that children learn not through words but through the energy and calmness we embody.

Raising a child with attentiveness today prevents wounds they must heal from later.

A Child's Requirements: The Simplicity of Love

A child asks not for perfection but for presence, security, and unconditional love.

Our own emotional and spiritual alignment impacts how safe and loved they feel.

Separation between parent and child carries weight, but the bond remains strong when nurtured with love and intention.

Dad's Matter: The Role of Fathers in a Child's Life

Fatherhood is a child's birthright; a father's presence shapes self-worth and resilience.

Lakota wisdom teaches that fathers play a vital role in guiding children through life's rites of passage.

The world must remember that a father's love is not secondary but foundational.

Sweet Child: A Message for the Next Generation

Children arrive with unfiltered love, curiosity, and magic; our role is to protect and nourish their spirits.

Indigenous teachings affirm that children carry ancient wisdom and must be guided with care, not control.

The world will try to harden them, but we must teach them another way – one of unity, kindness, and reverence for life.

Ode to Mothers: Honoring the Givers of Life

Mothers are the first home a child knows, the source of endless devotion and sacrifice.

Andean traditions honor the Pachamama, the Earth Mother, as the embodiment of nourishment and unconditional giving.

To appreciate our mothers is to carry their lessons forward in how we love and nurture our children.

Great Teachers: Living the Lessons We Share

True teachers do not instruct with words alone; they embody the lessons they teach.

Hopi wisdom teaches that great leaders guide through example, not control.

The way we live, move, and speak in our children's presence is the greatest lesson we offer.

The Cosmic Dandelion: Children Who Scatter Light

When raised in truth and alignment, children become seeds of wisdom, planting change wherever they go.

The Lakota believe children are sacred beings sent to remind us of our purpose.

A child nurtured in love does not seek external validation; they carry their light wherever they travel.

The Art and Power of Play

Play is vital for lifelong curiosity, health, and connection to the natural world – this is not only for children.

Indigenous cultures prioritize play as a means of learning, developing resilience, and regulating emotions.

Movement, laughter, and adventure connect us to our primal wisdom and keep our spirits alive.

Lions Gate Love: Honoring Transitions in Childhood

Growth is constant; children move through phases that must be honored, not feared.

A parent's role is to create a space where a child feels safe evolving and stepping into their own wisdom.

Every milestone offers an opportunity to affirm a child's strength, resilience, and divine purpose.

Protect What You Love: The Energy We Bring to Parenting

A child's environment shapes their nervous system, beliefs, and emotional well-being.

To raise a healthy child, we must embody health, peace, and clarity within ourselves.

Parents must shield children from toxic influences – whether chemical, energetic, or emotional – to allow them to thrive.

The Vastness of Pretty: Holding Reverence for Kids

Children are the continuation of our lineage; they carry the prayers of our ancestors.

Lakota traditions teach that children are divine gifts, meant to be nurtured, not controlled.

To honor a child is to recognize their infinite worth and treat them with the same reverence we show the sacred.

See God in Others: Honoring the Divine in Every Child

Every child carries a spark of the divine; to see them fully is to see God.

The Maya concept of *k'uxaaj*, the sacred heart, reminds us that children are born with deep knowing; our role is to guide, not impose.

When we raise children in truth, they move through the world knowing they are whole, powerful, and never alone.

Reflect & Apply Worksheet

1. Your Role in a Child's Life

How do you show up as a guiding presence for the children in your life?

What lessons have you inherited from your own upbringing that you wish to pass on – or break?

How can you be more present, patient, and intentional in your interactions with children?

2. The Power of Your Energy

Reflect on a time when your emotional state directly influenced a child's mood or behavior. What did you learn from this?

How do you regulate your energy to ensure children around you feel safe and nurtured?

What practices help you cultivate peace so you can lead by example?

3. Honoring the Sacredness of Childhood

How do you actively protect the purity and wonder of children in your care?

What distractions pull you away from presence, and how can you minimize them?

How do you encourage play, exploration, and curiosity in both children and yourself?

4. Fathers & Mothers as Pillars of Stability

How has the presence or absence of a father/mother figure shaped your understanding of family?

What does fatherhood/motherhood mean to you beyond biological ties?

5. Teaching Through Example

What personal habits do you want the next generation to emulate? Are you embodying them?

How can you practice greater alignment between what you teach and how you live?

What wisdom from the elders in your lineage would benefit children today?

6. Raising a Sovereign Child

How do you teach children to trust their own intuition?

What steps can you take to ensure children grow up with a strong sense of self-worth?

How do you help them navigate societal pressures while staying true to their essence?

7. Creating a Legacy of Love

If your child or a child in your life were to describe the lessons they learned from you, what would you want them to say?

What commitments will you make today to be a better teacher, guide, and protector?

Write a blessing, affirmation, or message to the next generation.

Final Reflection: Write a gratitude statement for the children in your life. How do they inspire you? How do they challenge you to grow?

Mantra for Integration: *I guide with love. I lead by example. I honor the divine in every child.*

Lesson X: Being a Good Person

"When we show our respect for other living things, they respond with respect for us." — Arapaho Proverb

Kindness is a language older than words, a force stronger than any law, a truth recognized by all living beings. The essence of each great teaching, every enlightened path, and all civilizations that have endured through time centers around altruism, benevolence, and grace.

To walk in a good way means more than avoiding harm. We are mindful of our presence, our footprint, and our duty to uplift others when they are in need. As we move through life, the goodness we put into the world protects us, shields us, and creates a path that is always illuminated.

Kindness holds a simple, yet profound power. Lao Tzu, the great sage of Taoism, taught: *"Kindness in words creates confidence. Kindness in thinking creates profoundness. Kindness in giving creates love."* Acts of kindness – whether small or grand – ripple outward, shaping not only the lives of those we touch but the very fabric of existence. A kind word can soften a heart, a generous hand can change a destiny, and life lived with integrity inspires generations.

In Indigenous traditions, kindness is not just a virtue but a law of nature. The Lakota people practice *Wówačhiŋtȟaŋka*, meaning *compassion and generosity without expectation.* To live this way is to be in harmony with all things – human, animal, land, and sky.

The Buddha also taught that kindness reflects true strength: *"A generous heart, kind speech, and a life of service and compassion are the things which renew humanity."* To be good is to be resilient, patient, and unwavering in the face of suffering. Weakness is a polarity to goodness. No one walks through life without error. Even the most enlightened stumble. What we do after we fall defines us. We are to overcome mistakes with humility and sincerity.

The Hopi people teach that mistakes are simply lessons along the path – opportunities to realign with our purpose. When we acknowledge our missteps with humility, when we make amends with sincerity, we cleanse ourselves and restore balance.

As the Bhagavad Gita reminds us: *"Perform every action with a pure heart, expect nothing in return, and you shall never be bound by regret."* A good person is not one who never falters, but one who chooses to rise again, always striving toward truth. There is a ripple effect of goodness in the world. Kindness does not end at the origin.

The smallest act – a meal shared, a door held open, a moment of listening – has the power to travel through time, shaping lives beyond what we will ever see. The Ubuntu philosophy of Africa teaches: *"I am because we are."* To be good is to recognize that we are woven into each other's existence. What we give to the world is what the world gives back to us.

The Hopi prophecy speaks of the time of great division, urging us to remember: *"This can be a good time. There is a river flowing now very fast. Those who cling to the shore will suffer. But those who let go, who step into the current with open hearts, will be carried to a new world."* This will be a world built on kindness, on service, on love. We will walk the path of goodness.

To be a good person is a practice, a way of being, not an achievement.

Harm no one.

Be mindful of your footprint.

Offer help when needed.

Be of service where you are called.

When we live with kindness, we walk through life protected, guided, and at peace. The universe does not forget those who move with love.

Reciprocity is in the Giving

"Do a good deed and throw this in a river. One day she will come back to you in a desert." — Rumi

True reciprocity is in the giving. The essence of kindness is not measured by what is returned but by the act alone, by the love infused in the offering. The Andean concept of *Ayni* teaches that reciprocity is a sacred exchange, an energy cycle that sustains balance – not through expectation, but through the natural order of life's flow. If we receive blessings in return, we honor the collective circulation of goodness and express gratitude; however, when we extend ourselves to ease another's burden, we must release all attachment to whether any correspondence is received.

There will be times when we pour into another, giving more than we knew we could, and what returns is not gratitude but rejection, not appreciation but betrayal. This too is a form of reciprocity – the universe showing us where others reside.

The lesson is to remain steadfast in goodness, to offer without expectation, and to trust that the integrity of our actions is enough. A mistruth spoken against us is an opportunity to embody honesty. A betrayal suffered is an invitation to deepen our trust in life's unfolding. Light simply exists, there is no struggle against darkness. In brightness, obscurity and shadows dissipate.

The elders of the Haudenosaunee Confederacy remind us: *"Give thanks for unknown blessings already on their way."* Reciprocity does not always return from the same hands we gave to, nor in the ways we imagined. Energy moves through the unseen, finding a way back in divine timing, in moments we least expect. The greatest gift we can offer anyone is prayer.

I pray for those who have wronged me, for those who are so lost in their own pain that they inflict hurt upon others. I ask Spirit to guide them toward healing, to reveal clarity where confusion clouds their hearts. I do not seek their redemption for my own sake, but for theirs – that they may once again recognize the goodness within them.

Perhaps the highest form of giving is kindness, and the beauty of this offering lies in the infinite ways this can be expressed. A listening ear, a warm meal, a word of encouragement, the unseen work of holding space for another. The Maya people speak of *Lak'ech Ala K'in – I am another you*. This principle reminds us that in lifting another, we lift ourselves. In healing another, we heal the collective. To give is to be in harmony with all life.

As those called to lead, we give as part of our nature, not for recognition. The joy that arises from an act of generosity is the only return we ever need. If we are taken advantage of, if our kindness is mistaken for weakness, we do not close ourselves off. Instead, we refine our discernment while keeping our hearts open. Love is not diminished by those who fail to receive; love is strengthened by those who continue to give despite this.

With time, we come to understand the complexities of human nature. We observe how people move through hardship, how they respond when they are forgiven for their betrayals, how even the most radiant souls have moments of shadow. We learn that to hold onto resentment is to poison our own spirit. As Mark Twain wrote, *"Anger is an acid that does more harm to the vessel in which stored than to the entity on which poured."* In community, we release this weight.

The Yoruba teach the wisdom of Òrìsà – divine forces that guide humanity, each representing an element of human experience. Among them is *Obatalá*, the orisha of wisdom, who reminds us that patience and clarity are the foundations of goodness. To act from love rather than reaction is to honor this wisdom, to move with intention rather than impulse.

The law of jiu-jitsu states: *"All energy directed at us is energy available for us."* When people direct any form of energy toward us – love, anger, admiration, resentment – we are given the power to transform this current any way we please. Will we meet hostility with hostility, or will we alchemize this into understanding? Will we let external forces dictate our nature, or will we remain unwavering in our truth?

This is our invitation to question humanity's role in the evolution of life on this planet. Are we here to command, conquer, and consume? Or are we in this position to restore, nourish, and uplift? Are we meant to mine, extract, and take, or to appreciate, protect, and preserve?

Reciprocity is about maintaining balance, not keeping score. The earth gives unconditionally – fresh water, fertile soil, air to breathe. The sun gives light without asking for repayment. May we learn to give in the same way, trusting that what we send into the world will always find a way home, not because we demand, but because the nature of the universe is to restore harmony to those who act with love.

Choose Ideal Idols: The Power of Influence

The people we admire shape who we become. The voices we listen to, minds we study, energies we allow into our sphere – they form the foundation of our thoughts, values, and actions. To choose our influences wisely is to take control of our own becoming.

Ancient wisdom teaches that we must be vigilant about who we allow to mold our perception of reality. The Yoruba tradition speaks of *Ori*, the inner head – the divine self-direction that, when cultivated, aligns us with destiny. When we follow false idols, when we allow shallow influences to dictate our beliefs, we stray from this path. But when we surround ourselves with integrity, wisdom, and those who carry truth in their words and deeds, we walk the way of righteousness.

Be disenchanted by what lacks vitality and sustenance. The world is saturated with voices demanding attention, yet few truly nourish the soul. Television, social media, and mainstream pseudo-culture feed distraction rather than depth. Toltec wisdom keepers taught that humanity lives in a collective dream – one that has been distorted by illusions. If we do not consciously shape our own dream, we will fall victim to the manufactured reality of those who seek to control our thoughts.

Most of the people I have idolized in my life are authors of old books who live on through the magic of their teachings and writings. Their wisdom is timeless, their influence enduring. They do not seek to entertain but to awaken. Their words do not fade with trends; they remain as guiding stars in the night sky of human understanding.

The people I adulate, and revere are original thinkers, wholesome educators, incorruptible leaders, bridge builders, difference makers – those who have the integrity to do what they say they will do with compassion and mindfulness. There are false prophets who subterfuge for profits. Trying to fit a square culture into an oval office. Pushing propaganda that is dishonest. I am not acquainted with the demons who haunt them.

Who we follow determines who we become. If you can lead me to unobstructed knowledge, help me decipher ancient codes, and guide me to primordial wisdom, I will forever be a loyal student. In Lakota tradition, wisdom is passed through oral teachings, each generation learning from the voices of those who walked before them. Knowledge keepers of the Dagara people of West Africa say that the elders are the *"libraries of the village,"* holding the truth of ancestral memory. In every culture rooted in truth, mentorship is sacred, and the quality of our mentors determines the trajectory of our path.

Our sphere of influence indicates our level of goodness. When we are influenced by good people, we have greater odds of becoming good ourselves.

If we study the lives of those who lived in alignment, we learn integrity.

If we seek teachers who embody wisdom, we learn discernment.

If we surround ourselves with those who practice patience, kindness, and purpose, we absorb these virtues into our own being.

The highest aim is not to idolize but to embody. To learn from the wise is not enough – we must integrate their wisdom so deeply that their teachings cease to be something we follow and instead becomes something we are. Beyond discipline, we simply become the embodiment of what is ours by divine right. From this place, we are impenetrable.

We must guard our minds as we guard our hearts. We must be deliberate in the voices we let shape our thoughts. Not all knowledge is wisdom, not all leadership is righteous, not all influence is pure. To align with truth, we must surround ourselves with truth. To become good, we must follow those who have walked the path of goodness before us. Choose wisely, and in time, become the guiding light for those who come after you.

The Weaponization of Decency: Truth to Restore Integrity

In a world where kindness is often mistaken for passivity, we are taught to suppress the truth under the guise of decency. We are conditioned to believe that confronting someone about the consequences of their choices is offensive, that holding others accountable is unkind. True love calls forth strength and does not coddle weakness. To see another's potential and remain silent as they self-destruct is neglect, not compassion.

The ancients knew that correction is an act of love. Yoruba tradition speaks of *Iwa Pele* – good character. To walk in good character is not to remain agreeable at all costs, but to uphold a balance of truth and integrity within the community. The Hopi believe that words carry the power to heal or to harm, and that silence in the face of another's suffering is a form of harm. The elders remind us there is no goodness in watching another descend into sickness, addiction, or degradation in the name of love.

When purity is lost, darkness takes root. *Beelzebub was a fallen angel who embodied a demon after being poisoned by his environment.* Angels and demons are not separate species – they are simply spirits fed differently. A being exposed to corruption, to toxicity, to distortion, will lose their radiance, their purity replaced with decay.

If the terrain is cleansed, blood is purified, and mind is freed from illusion, the angel resurrects. Holiness is simply buried beneath the weight of impurity, not lost forever. On a cellular level, this process is called pleomorphism. When a healthy cell is placed in an acidic, toxic environment, the cell mutates into a pathogen. When restored to an alkaline, nourishing state, the same cell functions optimally once more.

The human organism follows the same law. A person who is dependent on synthetic drugs, processed foods, and destructive habits is dimmed, their vitality eroded. Yet, when they cleanse their system, when they realign their choices, they shine again.

Real love holds up a mirror. We do not always have to see everyone in their highest light. To truly love is to recognize when someone has fallen from alignment and to tell them the truth. The weaponization of decency teaches us to bite our tongues, to avoid offending, to step aside as another spirals downward. This is not love. This is avoidance.

Yes, love can conquer all demons, yet love can also destroy when wielded without wisdom. How many times have we watched people harm themselves in the name of love? How often have we seen enablers feed destruction under the illusion of kindness? True love burns illusions away and does not indulge in them. To love in a way that empowers is to be direct, to be fearless, to be willing to provoke discomfort if discomfort leads to transformation.

The Tao Te Ching teaches: *"Give evil nothing to oppose and this force will disappear."* Yet, this does not mean we allow darkness to thrive unchecked. This teaches us not to fuel delusion with empty pleasantries. Sitting idly while someone poisons their body, their mind, and their spirit is to be complicit in their suffering. True compassion is intervention. True love is disruption.

To be good is not to be agreeable. To be kind is not to be silent. The challenge before us is to elevate the frequency of the collective by being authentic, by daring to say what is necessary rather than what is comfortable.

Do not inflate egos with words that protect illusion. Do not offer comfort that enables self-destruction. Speak the truth that others avoid, even at the risk of rejection. Love that does not challenge is love that does not serve.

May we provoke confrontation within those we care for, not to break them, but to shake them awake. May we remind each other that purity is always within reach, that the path home is never lost, only forgotten. May we always have the courage to guide those we love back to light, no matter the resistance we face along the way.

Do Not Engage in Divisive Rhetoric

There is a rampant and widespread endemic of people identifying as left or right, fragmenting themselves into ideological corners. They go so far as to classify even knowledge and wisdom as belonging to one extreme or the other. This is a distraction, a ploy to keep us from our center.

To remain whole, one must refuse to be pulled into these artificial battles. Why would anyone ever want to be anywhere but centered? Cultural engineers have conditioned society to cluster into opposing factions, to declare their ignorance as allegiance, and to fuel division. The lesson here is simple: **stay centered**.

When someone is fragmented and misaligned, they might attempt to break us – pulling us from our core because seeing us whole and undisturbed unsettles them. They will try to intoxicate our clarity, to shake our steadiness, to lure us into their turbulence. We have two choices: feed their demons by engaging, or remaining untethered, redirecting our energy toward noble and meaningful pursuits.

As we find our center and root in calmness and gentleness, distractions will come. The more we align with purpose, the more conflicting energies will attempt to disrupt us. These disruptions are not random; they are deliberate tests, invitations for us to demonstrate mastery over our emotions, impulses, and reactions.

If we falter – by allowing chaos to take root within us – we soon find ourselves in a recurring cycle. Different circumstances, same lesson. This will repeat until we transcend. The way forward is to become the observer, to recognize the patterns that draw us away from our equilibrium, and to master the art of non-engagement with division.

Identify the repetitive patterns that cause disruption, whether consciously or unconsciously.

Break these cycles with discipline, awareness, and detachment.

Return to your center when distractions arise, choosing composure over reaction.

Understand that advancing without mental delays requires unwavering focus on what truly matters.

Divisive rhetoric thrives on reaction. When we refuse to engage, we do not weaken; we fortify. By anchoring ourselves in clarity and stillness, we rise above the petty wars of ideology and ego, stepping instead into a space of true wisdom and discernment.

Ascend Through Humbleness: The Path to True Greatness

Humility is the highest expression of wisdom, the quiet power of those who walk in alignment with truth. To be truly good is not to proclaim oneself above another, but to live with such integrity that the presence of goodness speaks. True ascension is cultivated through the refinement of one's character, the shedding of illusion, and the surrender to higher harmonies. This is not calculated through status, wealth, or recognition.

Many Indigenous cultures understand that humility is not self-effacement, but self-awareness. The Navajo believe in *Hózhó*, the balance of beauty, harmony, and order within oneself and the universe. To live in *Hózhó* is to move through life with grace, to honor the sacredness in all things without seeking dominance.

The Buddhist path teaches the same – that ego collapses as consciousness expands, and the journey toward enlightenment is paved with humility, not pride. We never categorize ourselves as better. We simply live the best way we know and remain mindful enough to discern between good and bad, poison and health.

Distraction can act as a plague. With time we learn to discern what role attraction plays. Success comes when action is displayed. We find that forward movement is the direction our soul sways. As our purpose is conveyed, the pieces fit together, and spirit guides us to align with the violet flame. The shift from a lacking mindset to an abundant heart space.

We win the race when we bloom in the right place. We court the higher harmonies when we seal our energetic holes with grace. The gold that could never be mined awaits where our goals allineate with fate. We assemble creation to allocate all doubt and struggles into checkmate.

As our standards are raised, the pale face gets erased, insecurities fade, and uncertainties are replaced with surety. The depth with which we breathe drowns the shallow burrows of reluctance and hesitancy and we grant our aspirations the room they need to be conceived.

Moonstruck, building castles in the air, our losses capsized on sunken ships, nothing can plummet our ambitions – we are made for this. Collapse of ego expands our consciousness, and we rise from the declination of the dark abyss to ascend through humbleness.

There is a humble path to ascension. The wise do not seek superiority, only self-mastery. Elders teach that the greatest leaders are those who do not crave leadership. The most powerful beings are those who do not seek control. True mastery is to be so deeply rooted in purpose that comparison ceases to exist.

When we allow humility to be our compass, we:

Recognize that wisdom is endless and there is always more to learn.

Choose to uplift rather than overpower.

Understand that our personal growth is linked to the evolution of all beings.

A person who walks humbly does not need to prove their worth; their presence exudes value. They do not chase validation; they embody self-knowing. They do not hoard knowledge; they share freely, understanding that wisdom is a river meant to flow, not a possession to be locked away.

Tao Te Ching teaches, *"He who stands on tiptoe is not steady. He who rushes ahead does not go far. He who boasts will not endure."* The pursuit of ego is fleeting, but the path of humility is eternal. This is the gateway to higher consciousness, to peace beyond circumstances, to the quiet knowing that everything is unfolding exactly as intended.

To be truly good is not to seek goodness as an identity, but to allow decency, nobility, and righteousness to permeate our every action, thought, and word. As we relinquish the need for external validation, as we align with natural order, we rise – not by force, but by grace. This is the true ascension. This is the flowering of human consciousness.

May we all learn to bloom in the right place.

Key Takeaways from Lesson X

The Foundation of Goodness

Kindness is a force recognized across all civilizations and spiritual traditions.

The Hopi, Arapaho, and Lakota teachings emphasize harmony, respect, and service to others.

To be a good person is to be in alignment with truth, to uplift others, and to walk with integrity.

Reciprocity is in the Giving

True giving is not about receiving but about maintaining the cycle of goodness.

The Andean concept of *Ayni* teaches that reciprocity sustains harmony.

Betrayal and ingratitude are lessons that strengthen us; they do not diminish our goodness.

The highest form of giving is kindness, and prayer is an offering that transcends physical exchange.

The Power of Influence: Choosing Ideal Idols

Who we admire shapes who we become.

The Yoruba *Orí* (inner head) teaches that our influences determine our destiny.

Surrounding ourselves with wisdom and integrity ensures that we walk the path of righteousness.

Beyond discipline, we must integrate wisdom so deeply that we become the embodiment.

The Weaponization of Decency: Restoring Integrity

True love holds others accountable and does not enable self-destruction.

Yoruba *Iwa Pele* (good character) reminds us that silence in the face of suffering is a form of harm.
Love can be distorted when it is used to justify enabling poor choices.

To love in an empowering way is to challenge illusions and guide others back to purity.

Do Not Engage in Divisive Rhetoric

The current era thrives on division; remaining centered is the highest form of mastery.

Artificial battles distract us from true wisdom and clarity.

We must become observers, recognizing patterns that pull us away from our equilibrium.

Non-engagement with division strengthens our ability to walk in truth.

Ascend Through Humbleness: The Path to True Greatness

True mastery comes through humility, not dominance.

The Navajo *Hózhó* teaches balance, grace, and self-awareness.

The Tao Te Ching reminds us that boasting weakens and humility strengthens.

As we align with natural order, we rise – not by force, but by grace.

Reflect & Apply Worksheet

1. The Practice of Goodness

What does being a good person mean to you beyond societal expectations?

In what ways have you shown kindness this week without expecting anything in return?

How do you ensure your actions align with your values?

2. The Cycle of Reciprocity

Reflect on a time you gave freely and received an unexpected blessing in return.

How do you respond when kindness is met with betrayal or ingratitude?

What is one way you can practice *Ayni* (sacred reciprocity) in your relationships?

3. Evaluating Your Influences

Who are the five people (living or deceased) who influence your thinking the most?

Are these influences leading you toward greater wisdom, integrity, and peace?

What steps can you take to ensure you are surrounded by uplifting, truthful guidance?

4. Speaking Truth vs. Enabling

Have you ever remained silent to avoid discomfort, even when truth was needed?

How can you approach difficult conversations with both compassion and honesty?

What does this mean to you to love in a way that challenges, rather than enables?

1. Resisting Division & Staying Centered

What patterns of divisive thinking have you noticed in yourself or your environment?

How do you practice returning to your center when faced with conflict?

What strategies can help you remain composed and rooted in wisdom?

6. Humility as Strength

How do you define humility in contrast to self-deprecation?

What are some ways you practice quiet confidence rather than seeking validation?

How can humility serve as a foundation for your spiritual and personal growth?

Final Reflection: Write a personal statement on what being a good person means to you and how you will embody it moving forward.

Mantra for Integration: *I walk with kindness. I give without expectation. I stand in truth. I rise in humility.*

Lesson XI: Committing As a Loyal Lover

"Love is about appreciation, not possession." — Osho

To love is to honor, to protect, to show up fully. Loyalty is a sacred contract of presence, devotion, and unwavering integrity, not just a vow of exclusivity. Love, in highest form, is a sanctuary built on trust, not a battlefield of insecurities.

Across civilizations and throughout nature, loyalty has been the foundation of survival, unity, and harmony. From the great love stories of ancient kings and queens to the symbiotic partnerships in the plant and animal kingdoms, devotion is the force that holds all things together.

Loyalty is a way of being – a deep-rooted commitment to honor another, not just in words, but in action, in thought, in presence. There is sacredness in loyalty and transparency. Confucius, the great teacher of ethics, taught: *"To be trusted is a greater compliment than to be loved."* Love without trust is a house without foundation that crumbles under the weight of uncertainty. The ancient world revered loyalty not as an obligation, but as the highest expression of love.

In Ancient Egypt, love was considered sacred only when rooted in Maat – the principle of truth, justice, and order. A lover who deceived or strayed from integrity was believed to disrupt not just the relationship, but the balance of the cosmos. The Hopi people speak of love as a circle of reciprocity – to break loyalty is to break the cycle of life. The Celts saw love as eternal bonds, interwoven like the knots in their sacred art – unbreakable, unless dishonored.

Loyalty is a fierce commitment to show up, to protect, to cherish, to remain aligned in truth. This is about avoiding deception and hidden agendas and is not passive. The Bhagavad Gita reminds us: *"A man is made by his belief. As he believes, so he is."* A loyal lover does not indulge in secrecy, in hidden doors, in partial truths. They do not entertain temptation, for they know a fleeting pleasure is a poor trade for an eternal bond.

Temptation, at the core, is about ego, unfulfillment, and seeking externally what should be cultivated internally. This has nothing to do with attraction. A truly devoted lover is one who has done the inner work – who understands that fidelity is not a cage, but a choice made in clarity, respect, and deep reverence. We honor commitments in romantic relationships.

The animal kingdom is rich with examples of devotion and fidelity. Wolves mate for life, standing beside their chosen partner in loyalty, raising their young together, protecting their pack with unshaken integrity. Albatrosses return to the same mate, year after year, performing intricate dances to reaffirm their love. Gibbons form lifelong bonds, their trust solidified through song and touch, proving that love does not fade, but deepens.

In the fungal world, mycelium networks share nutrients, protect their connected trees, and foster a system of mutual growth and protection. Love is no different. A loyal lover does not drain or abandon – they nourish, they uphold, they protect.

In the bacterial world, symbiosis is survival. Just as bacteria and fungi form mutualistic relationships, love thrives in balance, reciprocity, and devotion. When both partners commit fully, they strengthen not only each other but the entire foundation of love.

There are complexities in devotion. Loyalty means choosing, every day, to honor a romantic bond in the highest form. This does not mean blind submission or staying in what does not serve. Love, when nurtured with truth, vulnerability, and unwavering presence, becomes an unshakable force – one that withstands storms, one that outlives time.

A loyal lover:

Speaks the truth, even when difficult.

Protects the sanctity of the union, never opening doors to dishonor.

Does not waver in devotion, even in the face of temptation.

Leads by example, embodying the kind of love that inspires generations.

Loyalty is the backbone of love – the thread that binds two souls across lifetimes. The legacy of devotion is written in the stars. Honor love. Honor trust. Honor the sacredness of devotion. For in the end, the promise we keep, even when no one is watching defines love – not possession, desire, or fleeting passion.

Overcoming Mistakes with Humility and Sincerity

There is no perfection in love, only devotion to growth. A relationship is not measured by the absence of mistakes but by the willingness to meet each misstep with humility, sincerity, and accountability. Love is practice, not performance.

The elders of the Quechua people say, *"A heart that carries blame cannot carry love."* The ability to own our mistakes is the foundation of trust. When we avoid accountability, when we shift blame or mask our errors in secrecy, we introduce shadows into the sacred bond. Transparency is the fabric from which trust is woven. This is not an option.

A loyal lover does not engage in shadiness or sketchy behavior. Love thrives in the light of understanding, patience, and the commitment to always choose clarity over concealment – not in deception. The Tao Te Ching teaches: *"A great nation is like a great man: When he makes a mistake, he realizes. Having realized, he admits. Having admitted, he corrects. He considers those who point out his faults as his greatest teachers."*

A strong relationship is built on:

Accountability – Taking ownership of our words, actions, and mistakes without deflection.

Vulnerability – Opening up about fears, wounds, and lessons learned rather than hiding behind pride.

Compassion – Understanding that imperfection is human and meeting errors with patience and grace.

When mistakes arise, a conscious lover does not react with anger or punishment but with inquiry: *How did we get here? What can we learn? How can we move forward with greater awareness?* There is no healing in guilt; there is only healing in understanding.

Love expands when nurtured with truth. The more we practice honesty, the deeper our connection becomes. The more we hold space for accountability, the more resilient our bond grows. A loyal lover does not seek perfection, but presence. They do not demand flawlessness, but sincerity.

To walk a path of devotion is to embrace the full spectrum of love – the beauty, the challenges, and the refining fire of growth. Mistakes will happen, but how we move through them defines the legacy of our love.

Courageous Love: The Art of Risk & Surrender

To love fully is to risk fully. True devotion requires an open heart, free from fear, free from contingency plans, free from attachments to safety nets. Love is meant to be embraced with absolute trust, not to be hedged. Rumi wrote, *"Be like a tree and let the dead leaves drop."* Love asks us to release fears of loss, heartbreak, or rejection, and instead surrender to divine selection. What is meant for us cannot be lost. What is not, will never stay.

A heart-protected cannot truly give, just as a bird tethered cannot soar. Love is an act of faith, a way to know that the universe brings us the person we need for our evolution. We do not bargain with fate. We receive love fully, trusting that the Creator orchestrates unions with purpose.

A lover who risks love lets go of fear and embraces presence. She does not keep back-up options but gives wholly. He trusts that love, when aligned, is indestructible.

To love courageously is to honor commitment and to walk forward, unguarded, knowing that every great love requires the willingness to risk everything. A truly devoted lover sees their partner not just as a person, but as a reflection of the sacred, and through this love, both ascend.

Sacred Devotion: Fidelity as an Act of Worship

Monogamy is a frequency, a sacred devotion to honoring the essence of one's beloved – not merely a structure. True fidelity is not a constraint, but a chosen depth, a pathway into divine union.

Monogamous is the taste of your lips.

The white wolf, as alpha dominant leader of his pack, is forever loyal to his queen. He only accepts her kiss.

A king swan rules in his mate's queendom and relates to her soul every waking moment. Her gold shines through his spirit.

Your heart is filled with earth tones.

I press up against the colors of redwood bark that emanate from your chest. Feeling your scars etch into my skin.

The sounds of angelic harps strum melodies that arouse life force from an abyss of dark.

When life gets hard, I am reminded of who you are. I get through another breath, one more day to start fresh. The warmth of your flesh. To be reborn in your depths.

I resurrect as a greater version of who I am, a better man, knowing I have walked in your lane. To have held your hand. To have been the recipient of your gaze.

Hercules is not as strong as the current you carry.

All the stars up in the sky are not as bright as your shine.

There are your verses in every song. The pieces of you in each strum. No lyrics have ever been sung that emulate the power of your wholeness undone.

Your smile. Your grin. The ancient light reflecting from your shoulders that will never dim.

The oceans are only as vast as the beauty you illuminate from within.

To be fully devoted is to recognize love as something far greater than desire. This is a sacred act, a merging of spirits, an alchemy of souls. The Bhagavad Gita teaches: *"That which is real never ceases to be."* Love is meant to be held with reverence, protected like fire, worshipped like the divine – not to be diluted, divided, or compromised.

The Sacred Act of Showing Up: Honoring Commitments

Love is not measured by grand declarations, but by the simple, consistent act of showing up. This is the daily commitment to presence, to honoring promises, to making space for another's heart as though our own.

The Apache people teach that true love is demonstrated in consistency – that words spoken must be matched by actions, and devotion must be shown through reliability. In the teachings of the Bhagavad Gita, Krishna emphasizes that duty and devotion go hand in hand. A love that is not honored through presence becomes a mere illusion.

A devoted lover does not:

Make promises they cannot keep.

Leave their partner questioning their commitment.

Withdraw when things become difficult.

Instead, they:

Stand firm, even in uncertainty.

Honor their partner's heart with patience and reverence.

Keep showing up, day after day, through the ordinary and the extraordinary.

Love thrives not in fleeting passion but in unwavering presence. A relationship built on showing up withstands storms, because both partners know they can trust in the foundation they have built together. Love, when honored with consistency, transforms into an unshakable force – one that deepens, evolves, and endures through all seasons of life.

Honoring the Feminine Divine

Love, in truest form, requires reverence for the sacred balance between the masculine and feminine. The feminine divine is not something to be possessed or controlled but to be honored, cherished, and upheld in her full radiance. She is the gateway to creation, the force that nurtures life, the essence of wisdom and intuition.

Throughout history, the divine feminine has been revered as the sacred force that guides the world toward healing and balance. The Maya honored Ix Chel, the goddess of fertility and medicine, as the bringer of intuition and life force. The Egyptians worshiped Hathor, the goddess of love and motherhood, as the embodiment of joy and divine connection. The Shakti energy of Hinduism represents the creative power of the universe, flowing through all that is vibrant and alive. To honor the feminine is to recognize her boundless influence, her strength, and the way she anchors love into form.

She resembles an orb. Her permanent glow. The lasting imprint she etched into my soul.

She is a shield that protects from cruelty's sharp sword. Her warmth heals my heart from the duress of being cold. My true north. The light that entices me to come back home.

The glimmer of her smile allures me to bring out my inner child. Her laugh is beguiling. Her energy tantalizes. There is an inexorable pull to come back to my center when I am enriched with her presence.

The greatest present one could ever receive. She is the gleaming force that could bring any man to his knees. The muse that all artists would forebear their riches just to see.

I could be chained with shackles and tied to a tree and her face will always set me free. Honeybees are envious of the potency of her nectar,
there is nothing more fragrant or sweet.

To truly love is to honor the feminine as divine, to protect her without controlling her, to uplift her without overshadowing her, to embrace her depths without fear.

An aligned man does not seek to suppress the feminine force, but to walk beside her, to learn from her, to nurture her as she nurtures all life. Hopi says, *"To touch the Earth is to touch the Mother,"* for all that sustains us is born from her. Love, when fully honored, is a sacred reciprocity – the balance of strength and softness, of power and grace, of presence and surrender.

To love in this way is to align with the divine plan – to step out of ego, to move beyond fear, and to recognize that in honoring love, we honor the very essence of life.

Transmuting Heartbreak: Returning to Purity and Trust

Not every love story unfolds in the way we imagined. Heartbreak is a fire that refines us, a force that asks us to surrender, to let go of attachment, and to trust in the greater design of the universe. The Tao Te Ching reminds us: *"New beginnings are often disguised as painful endings."* Love lost is transformed, not wasted love. Our experiences of loss are not meant to harden us, but to teach us deeper faith, deeper patience, deeper surrender to the divine plan.

Heartbreak, if not transmuted, can become a weight that drags us away from our own center. If we internalize rejection, if we allow grief to dictate our self-worth, we sever our connection to divine love. Love is about alignment, never about ownership. If something is taken from us, this no longer serves our highest good.

To transmute heartbreak is to remain rooted in purity. We accept pain without allowing hardness to corrupt our goodness. We feel grief without distorting our capacity to love again. The Bhagavad Gita teaches: *"The soul is neither born nor dies; and is not slain when the body is slain."* Love, like the soul, is eternal. The force changes form but never disappears.

A heart aligned with *The Way Knows* does not seek vengeance, or act out of spite, and does not close off from future love. Instead, she remains open, trusting that all things return in divine timing.

To truly heal, we must:

Remain centered – Never allow another's actions to pull us from our own alignment.

Trust the divine plan – What is meant for us will find us when we are ready.

Dissolve attachment – Love evolves; does not end in loss.

Return to purity – No rejection or pain should make us bitter or closed off.

The universe does not remove love to punish us; space is cleared for something different. A warrior of love does not retreat in fear but stands in unwavering faith. When love is lost, we do not collapse, we rise, we learn, we walk forward with greater clarity.

Heartbreak is an initiation, not an ending. The more we trust, the more we receive. The more we remain open, the more love finds us. When found, we welcome with full, radiant, unwavering presence.

Key Takeaways from Lesson XI

Love as Honor, Not Possession – True love is built on appreciation, trust, and unwavering integrity rather than control or insecurity.

Loyalty as a Sacred Contract – Loyalty is not just about exclusivity but about presence, devotion, and truth. A lover's commitment must be reflected in action, thought, and energy.

Lessons from Ancient Civilizations – In cultures like Ancient Egypt and the Hopi tradition, love was considered sacred only when rooted in truth, justice, and cosmic balance.

Nature's Devotion – Loyalty is evident in the animal and fungal kingdoms, where lifelong bonds, mutual nourishment, and protection reflect the divine design of commitment.

Fidelity as a Conscious Choice – A loyal lover does not indulge in secrecy or entertain temptation. Fidelity is not a cage but a chosen depth of connection and reverence.

Overcoming Mistakes with Humility – Love is strengthened through accountability, vulnerability, and compassion. Trust is built through consistent honesty and transparency.

Courageous Love: Risk and Surrender – To love fully is to trust completely. Love is an act of faith, requiring an open heart free from fear.

Sacred Devotion as Worship – Monogamy, in highest form, is a frequency of devotion, not just a societal structure. Love is a merging of spirits and an alchemy of souls.

The Sacred Act of Showing Up – True devotion is shown through consistency, presence, and honoring commitments beyond mere words.

Honoring the Feminine Divine – Love requires reverence for the sacred balance between the masculine and the feminine. The feminine is to be cherished, not possessed.

Transmuting Heartbreak – Loss and heartbreak are transformative forces meant to refine, not to close the heart.

Reflect & Apply Worksheet

1. Self-Reflection:

What does loyalty mean to you in the context of love and commitment?

Have you ever mistaken possession for devotion? How did this affect your relationships?

Reflect on a time when you showed unwavering loyalty. What motivated this commitment?

2. Awareness & Action:

In what ways can you cultivate deeper trust in your relationship(s)?

How do you respond to temptation, and what internal work can you do to reinforce commitment?

What actions demonstrate your devotion and presence beyond verbal affirmations?

3. Nature's Guidance:

Choose an example from nature (e.g., wolves, albatrosses, mycelium networks) that reflects commitment. What lessons can you integrate from this into your love life?

How does reciprocity play a role in maintaining trust and balance in love?

4. Overcoming Mistakes:

Reflect on a mistake you've made in a past or present relationship. How did you approach accountability and repair?

What steps can you take to create an environment of transparency and growth in your relationship?

5. Devotional Love Practices:

Write down three ways you can show up consistently for your partner.

How can you honor your partner's essence in a way that uplifts them without seeking control?

Consider writing a letter to your partner (or future partner) about your commitment to love as a sacred act.

6. Transcending Heartbreak:

If you have experienced heartbreak, how have you transmuted the pain into wisdom?

What beliefs about love need to be released so you can open your heart again?

How can you cultivate faith in divine orchestration when love does not unfold as expected?

Use this worksheet as a guide for deeper introspection and application of the principles of loyalty, trust, and sacred devotion in love. *The Way Knows* that love, when honored, becomes an indestructible force of cosmic alignment.

The 4th Realm: Unifying with Spirit

Lesson XII: Choosing Spirit & Remaining Centered

"When we are centered in ourselves, nothing can disturb our peace. The whole universe may shift, yet the one who is anchored in spirit remains unshaken." — Lao Tzu

To remain centered is to stand unshaken in a world that seeks to pull us apart. We choose spirit over illusion, stillness over chaos, wisdom over distraction. The modern world was engineered to fracture, scatter, and disconnect us – from nature, from truth, from ourselves. But when we return to stillness, to breath, to spirit, we reclaim the guidance that has always been leading us.

The Indigenous peoples of this Earth have long known that to be rooted in spirit is to be rooted in life. To be present, whole, and deeply attuned to the rhythm of existence. In Lakota wisdom, the phrase *"Nake nula waun welo"* means *"I am always ready, at all times, for anything that may come."* This readiness is not about control but about trusting the way.

Tao Te Ching teaches: *"To the mind that is still, the whole universe surrenders."* When we cultivate stillness, we align with the Great Way. We become like the ancient trees, the flowing rivers, the mountain peaks – firm in presence, yet flexible to the unfolding of life. In a world of noise and urgency, stillness is an act of revolution. This is the refusal to be pulled into distraction, into fear, into the currents that seek to dismantle our clarity.

The Hopi people speak of the river that moves swiftly, warning that those who cling to the shore will suffer. Instead, they urge: *"Let go of the shore, push off into the middle of the river, keep your head above water, and see who is there with you."* Stillness is the clarity that allows right action to emerge. The warrior in the storm does not fight the wind but moves together with this vital force in synergy.

In Indigenous traditions, breath is considered sacred medicine. Breath can be utilized for returning to our center. The breath is our direct tether to spirit, the only constant rhythm we carry from birth to death. Yogis teach that breath is prana, or life force, a bridge between the physical and divine.

Many tribes, including the Diné (Navajo), teach that breath carries the song of our ancestors, that to breathe with awareness is to call upon their wisdom. When we lose ourselves, we return to breath. Slow inhales root us in the present. Deep exhales release what is not ours to carry. Pauses between breaths remind us that silence, too, is part of the rhythm.

The way the wind moves through the valleys and canyons is the way the breath moves through our being – guiding us home, again and again. We are encouraged to trust that a divine presence is always guiding us. The modern world has conditioned us to distrust the unseen, to worship only what can be measured, but our ancestors knew better. They listened to the language of the trees, the whispers of the fire, the rhythms of the animal kingdom.

Mycelium networks carry wisdom beneath the soil, transmitting nutrients between trees, proving that even in darkness, connection remains. Wolves follow instinct, never doubting the hidden force that pulls them home. Birds migrate thousands of miles, guided not by maps but an inner knowing. Humans, however, although thought to have been given the most awareness, have been taught to question their own intuition.

Lakota people have a saying: *"The longest journey you will make in your life is from your head to your heart."* Trust that you are being led, always. Not by the world's distractions, but by the same force that moves the stars, turns the tides, and speaks through winds and rivers. Reindigenization is returning to the root of being.

The culture we have been given is not our true culture. Modern society was built to sever us from the land, from ritual, from deep listening. This diversion from nature was designed to separate us from spirit – to keep us uncentered, consuming, distracted. To return to our indigenous wisdom is about reclaiming our right to be in harmony with nature, to honor the sacred in all things. This goes beyond ethnicity, nationality, or race.

The way forward is not found in more technology, more artificial intelligence, or more mindless consumption. The way forward is found in slowing down, deepening our breath, standing barefoot on the land, and remembering songs of Earth.

To remain centered is to refuse to be swayed by illusion. To choose spirit is to walk the path of the wise. Breathe. Listen. Be still and know – the way has always been within you.

Reindigenization: Restoring Sacred Balance

"All people started out as Indigenous. Everybody has a right and responsibility to look at the way colonization has occurred through patriarchy, and with patriarchal thinking. People must know that Indigenous knowledge resides in the deeper layers of their consciousness. We need rituals and exercises to peel away the false effects of colonialism and get down to our natural self." — Yoruban Grandmother, Yeye Luisah Teish

Reindigenization is remembering, restoring, and embodying ways of living that align with the natural world. This can be remembered as a reclamation of wisdom lost to colonialism, the renewal of kinship with land, and the healing of fractures created by imposed systems seeking to sever us from our roots.

With advancements in technology and transportation, food can be grown and distributed across all regions, knowledge can be shared instantly, and resources exist to shelter and nourish all people. Yet rather than living in harmony with this abundance, modern society clings to scarcity, control, and disconnection. The colonial mindset has disrupted humanity's relationship with Earth, replacing reverence with exploitation. The Indigenous way of thinking – one rooted in reciprocity, humility, and responsibility – has been suppressed in favor of domination.

The western world's addiction to excess and consumption is a stark contrast to the Indigenous mind, which is shaped by balance and deep respect for all life forms. As we witness cultures fading, languages vanishing, and native lands being exploited, we must turn to the wisdom keepers who remind us that regeneration is possible. This is the flowering of reindigenization.

Native Lineage: Reconnecting with Ancestral Wisdom

Wade Davis, an ethnographer who has spent his life documenting Indigenous cultures, warns in *The Wayfinders*, *"Anthropologists predict that fully fifty percent of the seven-thousand languages spoken around the world will disappear within our lifetimes."* Each language lost is a doorway to an entire worldview collapsing – songs, stories, medicine, and ways of knowing erased forever.

What defines your culture? How can we ensure that the knowledge we hold is inherited by future generations? How do we preserve the stories, songs, and sacred ways of our ancestors? These questions call us to examine our place within the greater web of existence. To neglect native traditions is to sever our connection to who we are at our core.

As Gikuyu scholar Ngugi Wa Thiong'o writes, *colonization of the mind happens when we allow foreign narratives to dictate our understanding of ourselves.* Vandana Shiva further explains that *a monoculture of the mind leads to monocultures in the fields – sterile, lifeless, and incapable of sustaining diversity.*

To reindigenize is to remember that we are all, at some point in time, native to a land, a way of life, a rhythm that once flowed in harmony with the natural order. The return to this knowing is not about race or nationality, but about restoring relationships – with the Earth, with each other, and with the unseen forces guiding us.

Lyla June Johnston speaks of this beautifully: *"Regenerative agriculture is not only about regenerating soils. This is also about healing relationships, healing history, healing the people who still languish in the shadows of the legacies of colonization."* Healing the land is healing the self. Healing the self is healing the lineage. Healing the lineage is healing the future.

In Māori tradition, two fundamental questions are asked:

Ko wai au? – Who am I?

No wai au? – Whom do I come from?

These questions form the foundation of a life lived in integrity.

Who are you, beyond imposed identities and conditioned beliefs? Who are your ancestors, and what values did they uphold? What forces pulled your lineage away from native ways? What will you do to reclaim, restore, and revitalize what was lost?

To answer these questions is to walk in awareness of our place within history. We honor those who came before us by ensuring that their wisdom is woven into the fabric of our daily lives. Reciprocity is the essence of indigenous living. Indigenous cultures teach that nothing is separate – what we take, we must give back. What we consume, we must regenerate. This is the law of reciprocity. The soil, the trees, the rivers, and the animals are not resources to be exploited, but relatives to be honored.

Ohiyesa, from the Wahpeton Santee Sioux tribe, reminds us that *materialism is a sickness that disturbs spiritual balance*. He urges that children must be taught early the beauty of generosity, for clinging to possessions is to weaken the spirit.

As we reindigenize, we embrace the practices that sustain life rather than deplete:

We listen to the land. We grow food with reverence, not greed. We recognize plants and animals as teachers, not commodities.

We return to ritual. Ceremony is a bridge between worlds, grounding us in presence and gratitude.

We reclaim native tongues. Language shapes thought, and through words, entire cosmologies are preserved.

We honor kinship. Family extends to the community, the Earth, and all living beings, and goes beyond blood ties.

We live with intentional simplicity. We consume only what is needed and recognize the true wealth in spiritual alignment.

Reindigenization is a return home, not a trend or a movement. This represents the peeling away of layers of colonization, the unlearning of harmful conditioning, and the reawakening of ancestral memory. We are reminded that we are stewards, not owners. Earth does not belong to us – we belong to the Earth.

To remain centered is to refuse the distractions that pull us from this truth. To choose spirit is to walk the path of those who came before us, whose wisdom still hums beneath the soil, in the rivers, in the whisper of the wind.

Reindigenization is remembering, restoring, and returning. Let us walk this path with reverence. Let us reclaim what was stolen, restore what was broken, and rise as guardians of the sacred.

Aid From Our Ancestors

Our ancestors are always rooting for us. They are spiritual warriors going to battle for us in celestial court every time we make a mistake, commit a wrong, or say or do anything unaligned. When we tell them what we want, and vocalize to them where we have been wrong, they will work in our favor to smooth things out and help us manifest what we are envisioning. There is no reason to feel shame or guilt about something when we can leave this for them to resolve. We simply need to trust them.

Being honest with ourselves is being transparent with them. They see what we are up to. They know what we are capable of and want more than anything for us to be good people, to succeed, and to carry compassion with our walk. We are ancestrally bound to the experiences that allowed us to be here today. We inherit their songs, stories, and wisdom, yet we also write our own. We choose what we keep, and what we let go of. With each generation, our awareness expands, and consciousness grows.

This is our opportunity to make them proud – not by repeating every imprint they left, but by correcting missteps, breaking faulty cycles, and evolving our lineage. Our ancestors do not wish for us to carry their burdens; they wish for us to refine what was given and elevate our collective spirit. To heal, to break cycles, to choose wisdom over inherited wounds – this is how we honor them. This is how we create a lineage that is more aligned, more whole, more luminous. They do not expect us to walk their exact path, but to walk forward, carrying the best of them while forging something even greater.

Redefining Culture

"The boundaries we erect to divide heaven from earth, mind from matter, real from unreal are mere conveniences. Having made the boundaries, we can unmake them just as easily." — Deepak Chopra

Culture is a living, breathing force shaped by the aspirations and actions of a people – not a fixed structure. To redefine culture is to reclaim what nourishes growth and integrity while discarding what no longer serves. The modern world has engineered a culture of distraction, deception, and disconnection.

The corporate-designed education system distorts history, politics are rooted in mistruths, and propaganda shapes the aspirations of men. We have been conditioned into a culture of consumption, numbed by entertainment, poisoned by destructive habits, and distanced from wisdom. We are not bound by these constructs, though. Culture is cultivated like soil and must be tended with care, aligned with truth, and made fertile for evolution.

We have the power to counterprogram, to foster a culture rooted in wisdom, honor, and authenticity. We can step outside of screens, research beyond mainstream narratives, reclaim our physical and mental health, and choose community over isolation.

True culture emerges from the land, from the soul, from the depth of our being – not from corporations or institutions. To redefine culture is to return to what nourishes us, reject the walking-dead culture of addiction and distraction, and foster an existence of clarity, purpose, and connection.

This is the time to break away from what weakens us. To embody an unshakable resilience, to redefine strength beyond fragility, to mature into wisdom, and to shape a cultural paradigm that honors life. We are being called to cultivate something greater. Let us rise to that call.

In dominant culture, change is often implemented through force, coercion, and manipulation. True transformation, however, comes through alignment – ceremony, discipline, connection, and deep reverence for divine orchestration.

We do not impose change upon reality; we co-create with seasons. We do not extract what is not ours; we trust that what is meant for us will find us. This path omits the need for entitlement, removes illusions of control, and surrenders to unfolding of spirit.

Buddha taught that our experiences are mirrors of our mindset. What we focus on, we manifest. Our thoughts, beliefs, and intentions act as energetic magnets, shaping the trajectory of our lives. When we develop a pure connection with spirit, we manifest from a place of clarity, rooted in our highest potential rather than our wounds.

Walking the Path: Becoming the Embodiment of Light

I once received guidance from an elder who gave me three virtues to live by:

Believe in your heart – Remember that everything exists within you. Stand before a mirror and say, *"I love you, God,"* for the divine lives within you.

Live in joy – Laugh, play, make jokes, and find the lightness in life. Do not allow the weight of the world to rob you of your spirit.

Honor your worth – Keep track of what you are doing, ensure you are walking with purpose, and align yourself with what you truly desire.

No longer can we permit ourselves to act out unconscious patterns. No longer can we justify actions that do not serve our highest calling. The path is before us, illuminated by those who came before, waiting for us to take the step.

The warrior of light does not shrink in the face of darkness. They remain untouched, steadfast, and whole – never allowing those who lack connection to spirit to penetrate their shield of goodness. Let them scoff. Let them sneer. Let them mock what they do not understand. We will rise, untouched, unwavering, illuminated.

Taming the Demons: Alchemizing Darkness into Light

Learn your demons' names. This is a spiritual world, and over time we attract entities that move with the energy we feed them. These forces are neither good nor bad; they merely follow the current we set. If we indulge in toxicity, whether through food, thought, or action, we create a shadowed path. But darkness, when acknowledged, always moves toward light.

To hold a clean space, we must walk a path of purity and guide all energies in our field toward illumination. Any dis-ease, whether spiritual or physical, stems from misalignment. To heal, we must guide even our deepest shadows into the light.

The snake sheds her skin with the help of a rock, a tool gifted by nature to aid in transformation. So too must we use the tools available to us – ritual, discipline, love – to evolve beyond what seeks to confine us.

The world is filled with those who mock wisdom and scoff at sincerity. Their detachment blinds them, and their privilege keeps them from seeing the depth of reality. But we do not have to let them in. A strong heart shines so brightly that darkness cannot enter – and does not absorb the bitterness of the world. The warrior of light does not engage in petty battles or waste energy convincing those who do not wish to see. Instead, they remain radiant, untouchable, and unwavering in their goodness.

When we elevate our frequency, we must protect our energy. To engage in lower vibrations, whether through toxic relationships, substances, or distractions, is to lower ourselves to a plane that does not serve us. The goal is not just to rise but to bring others with us.

We uplift through presence, humor, and joy. Every interaction is an opportunity to imprint goodness into the world. How we show up each day becomes our mantra. We construct an impenetrable shield around our sphere and reflect confusion and insecurity back as clarity and strength. We do not crumble; we become golden.

Artisan's Hands: The Bridge Between Spirit and Creation

"With our hands, we serve, we heal, we create. They are the instruments of our heart's intent, shaping the world with each touch." – Khalil Gibran

A teacher once shared, *"The hand that harms is also the hand that heals."* With our hands, we shape the world, create, nurture, and uplift – or we destroy, neglect, and withhold. The power to choose rests within us.

I am grateful for these hands I have been blessed with. They have always been catalysts for service, for manifesting vision, for embracing life. As a child, I held onto my mother and father with these hands; today, I hold my own children with the same hands. I have healed and strengthened others through bodywork, fitness, and nourishment. I have held my lover with passion, tenderness, and strength. I have created; I have destroyed. My hands know both the light and the shadow.

My hands have also been folded in prayer – seeking forgiveness, wisdom, and protection. They have rested on earth, touching the soil, planting seeds, stirring the sacred elements of creation. Hands are not merely tools; they are conduits of energy, vessels of intention, bearers of destiny.

I pray that these hands may always be instruments of goodness – that they bring healing where there is pain, nourishment where there is lack, and creation where there is potential. May my hands be blessed with the wisdom to build, to comfort, to guide, and to serve. May they carry love in all they touch.

Let us honor the gift of our hands, for they are not separate from spirit but extensions. Through them, we shape reality. Through them, we honor life.

The Power of Stillness in Turbulent Times

Stillness is the presence of profound awareness, not the absence of movement. When the world rushes, the wise stand still. This has been the way of mystics, sages, and warriors for millennia. In times of turmoil, those who remain centered become the anchors for all around them.

The samurai of ancient Japan understood that stillness was the foundation of mastery. A warrior did not react to chaos but instead moved, when necessary, guided by deep presence and precision. Miyamoto Musashi, the legendary swordsman, wrote, *"If you know the way broadly, you will see a path in all things."* To be unmoved by external noise is to wield true power.

In Taoist traditions, the still pond reflects the moon. A restless mind distorts reality, while a tranquil mind sees with clarity. The Buddha sat beneath the Bodhi tree in absolute stillness as Mara – the embodiment of illusion – tempted him with fear and desire. He remained unmoved, anchored in knowing, and thus awakened.

In Vedic philosophy, the concept of *sthita-prajña* refers to one who is unwavering in wisdom, regardless of external circumstances. The Bhagavad Gita teaches that the one who is centered in truth remains serene in the face of both pleasure and pain, gain and loss, praise and blame.

When all around us is chaos, trust that there is a greater force holding everything together. Birds do not question migration – they follow an invisible current of knowing. Wolves do not hesitate on their path home. The mycelium beneath the soil communicates wisdom across vast distances, unseen yet undeniable.

Likewise, we are always being guided. Our guidance is not heard in frantic movement but is received in stillness. The Tao Te Ching reminds us: *"The way is not in action but in quiet contemplation. The sage does nothing, yet nothing is left undone."* The modern world urges urgency, but wisdom remains still. The wise listen, breathe, and surrender. For in that stillness, the truth is revealed.

Five Ways to Remain Still and Centered

Breathe as the Trees Breathe – Breath is a bridge between body and spirit. In yogic teachings, deep diaphragmatic breathing (pranayama) calms the nervous system and returns us to presence. A slow inhale expands awareness, a deep exhale releases tension. We breathe with intention to remain steady in storms, just as trees synchronize with seasons.

Embody the Stillness of Water – Water teaches us the power of receptivity and flow. A river moves around obstacles, finding the path of least resistance. Stillness does not mean rigidity; this interprets learning when to be like the ocean's depth rather than the surface waves. The Tao Te Ching states: *"Nothing in the world is as soft and yielding as water, yet for dissolving the hard and inflexible, nothing is more efficient."*

Anchor in the Eternal Present – Past and future are illusions that create suffering. Zen teachings emphasize the practice of mindfulness – being fully here, fully now. Breath, sensation of wind on skin, the rhythm of the heart – these are the only real moments. Thich Nhat Hanh reminds us, *"The present moment is filled with joy and happiness. If you are attentive, you will see."*

Listen to the Silence Between Sounds – True wisdom is found not in noise but in the spaces between. Many Indigenous traditions revere silence as the greatest teacher. The Lakota once taught that silence was the heartbeat of creation, and the Zen koans often lead students to enlightenment through paradox and stillness. When the world shouts, listen instead to the quiet.

Surrender to the Great Flow – To trust spirit is to let go of control. The river moves with the currents of divine orchestration without questioning the route. Hindu philosophy speaks of *Ishvarapranidhana*, surrendering to the divine. Those who release attachment to outcome and allow themselves to be guided by spirit remain centered, no matter how wild the storm.

Breaking Cycles: Eluding Patterns of Fear and Scarcity

Richard Rudd writes in *The Gene Keys*, "*When you raise the frequency beyond the reach of concepts such as success and failure, you remember that all of life moves in a great cosmic pattern. As you let go into this pattern, you always find your natural support within.*"

The key to breaking patterns is in heightening frequency. We begin by identifying what depletes us. Fear, worry, and self-imposed limitations confine us to scarcity. Our first step is to shift away from lack-based thinking and into abundance.

What we ingest – mentally, physically, and spiritually – determines our frequency. Breaking patterns requires rejecting what is unnatural: dependency on substances, addiction to processed foods, immersion in artificial entertainment. These habits fragment our being and weaken our alignment.

To transcend limiting cycles, ask yourself:

What thoughts or habits are lowering my frequency?

How can I realign with a path of nourishment and clarity?

Where in my life can I replace depletion with renewal?

When we free ourselves from these entanglements, we reclaim our vitality.

Oneness: The Illusion of Separation

Science now confirms what ancient wisdom has always known – beneath our perceived differences, we are one. We can now use biometrics to confirm our identity from the shape, size, and beat of our hearts. No two heartbeats are the same. Wavelengths generated from the contractions and expansion of our heart are distinct enough to tell us apart from others.

Of the several billion humans occupying this planet, each of us carries a unique face. The patterns on our fingertips are woven to different rhythms, no two alike. We are the only match for our DNA. Despite these individual certainties, a University of California study confirmed that when two people rise in love, their heartbeats begin to synchronize. Our DNA can even live inside our partners. Over time, couples start to resemble each other.

Her scars get etched into his skin. His fingers become part of her hands. Did she just laugh, or was that him? What this reveals is that the boundaries we construct between ourselves and others are illusions. We are intertwined – not just with each other, but with all of life. Our existence is a song, played in harmony with the universe. We inhale the breath of trees, and in return, they drink in the air we exhale. We touch the earth, and in doing so, we touch the body of the divine.

The Myth of Human Supremacy

Western thought has long upheld the illusion of human supremacy – the belief that humankind exists apart from, and above, all other life forms – but this is a distortion. Indigenous wisdom teaches that divinity is not confined to human form. Lakota tradition speaks of *Wakan Tanka*, the Great Mystery, an ever-present force that loves all unconditionally.

Throughout history, cultures have carried interpretations of creation – from the story of Skywoman landing on Turtle Island to the Christian narrative of Jesus as the divine manifestation of God. Yet, to assume that the creator was only embodied in human form is to ignore the vast intelligence of existence.

God has lived as a wolf, a jaguar, a cedar tree, a mountain stream. Divinity is not bound by one species, one story, or one form. This Great Spirit rides on hawk wings through the vast sky and dangles on yellow aspen leaves that dance in autumn sun. This energy instructs seeds to germinate, sprout, and blossom into fruits, plants, and trees that sustain all life. Every step upon unscathed forest soil massages the soul of God resting in each atom of nature.

To believe that humankind alone carries divine wisdom is to be blind to the sacred intelligence that moves through all beings. The same force that whispered scripture into the minds of prophets also teaches a salmon the upstream route, tells an eagle how to ride the wind, and guides the moon in her cycles.

When we recognize this, our understanding of the divine expands. We no longer see the world as something to conquer, but as something to learn from. We begin to walk gently, to listen deeply, to approach life with reverence.

The presence of the divine within us flourishes when we create a terrain of purity for this force to inhabit. When we ingest impurities – whether through food, our actions, or thoughts – we distance from our highest potential. The further we stray from nature, the more we struggle to hear the voice of spirit.

To return to alignment, we must cleanse our body, mind, and heart. We must listen to the wisdom of the earth, of animals, of the elders who have not forgotten the sacred way. We must remember that every being carries a piece of the divine, and honoring them, we honor ourselves.

There is no polarity to divinity. This force does not belong to one species or one doctrine. We refer to the breath of wind, the pulse of oceans, hum of the bee, the rhythm of our hearts. The illusion of separation dissolves when we step outside of human-centered thought and embrace the oneness that has always been.

To remain centered is to remember this truth. To choose spirit is to recognize the sacred in all things, and to walk the path of the wise is to live in harmony – not above the world, but as a part.

The Polarity of Creation: Destruction or Transformation

We are all creators, whether recognized or not. The polarity of creation is destruction – when we are not actively creating, we often unconsciously destroy. We allow our energy and time to be eroded when we engage in habits that weaken our spirit: the abuse of substances, indulgence in meaningless distractions, unhealthy relationships, excessive consumption, and attachment to temporary pleasures.

This is an invitation to be wise and get clear about what you are creating. Are you building something with sustenance that will bring you abundance, joy, and fulfillment? Or are you feeding distractions, investing in what drains your essence? Be transparent with yourself about what you are seeking. Destruction and creation are always in motion – choose to create with intention.

The etymological meaning of the word *allergy* is *"altered reactivity."* When viewed through this lens, we are all susceptible to allergies – not just physical, but spiritual. Distractions, harmful lifestyle habits, poor nutrition, and unhealthy thoughts all lead to a shift in receptivity. These are not simply external irritants but internal distortions, depleting our vitality and interfering with our alignment.

If we know certain people, places, and habits trigger allergenic responses in our soul – why do we continue to expose ourselves? Just as we avoid food allergens to protect the body, we must avoid toxic influences to protect the spirit. This is your invitation to let go of people who lower your standards and habits that make less of you. They could be blocking your path to ascension.

To cultivate wholeness is to breathe deeply, live intentionally, and remember – always – your infinite connection to the source of all things.

Wholeness of Spirit: Returning to Fullness

Shifting away from wholeness when we experience feelings of inadequacy or incompleteness is easy when we are not disciplined and lack discernment and faith. To feel love in the way that God feels love, we must fill our voids – not with external distractions, but with presence, awareness, and connection. Love is only achieved in a state of fullness. So, we surrender our emptiness, allowing the universe to enrich us with true nourishment.

Reduction in vitality leads to diminution of spirit. Both result in a weakened energetic state, and both must be consciously restored. Our spirit is the life force within us, manifested in the way we express ourselves. Character reflects the quality of our spirit – how we speak, act, and navigate the world.

To restore energy, we sanctify breath. Oxygen is the bridge between vitality and spirit. Conscious breathing increases life force, clears stagnant energy, and revitalizes the mind. Just as trees exhale what we inhale, and we exhale what they inhale, we are in constant exchange with the living world. When we breathe deeply, we return to the sacred rhythm of existence.

The Illusion of Smallness: Refusing to Disappear

We are asked to release the lesser things in life and focus on what holds true and lasting value. Acting small to secure a sense of belonging is a forfeiture of purpose, not a noble move. Lao Tzu said, *"The way to do is to be."* Be the person you have always needed. Be the change you pray to see. Be the calm that soothes chaos. Be the remedy when tending to those who are broken. Be the nurturer who lifts them back up. Become the higher frequency.

What we share with all living beings is the innate desire to exist, to thrive, to evolve. At the end of each day, the King and the pawn return to the same box. Choose not to subscribe to illusions of hierarchy or limitation – rise into the truth of your boundless potential. To remain centered is to recognize the polarity of creation and destruction, to choose transformation over depletion, and to embody ethical change. To choose spirit is to release what weighs you down and step fully into your divine potential.

Key Takeaways from Lesson XII

Stillness as Strength – True power comes from stillness, not reaction. To remain centered is to stand firm in the face of chaos.

Breath as a Spiritual Bridge – Breath connects us to spirit, guiding us home in moments of disconnection. Conscious breathing restores clarity and presence.

Breaking Cycles – To elevate our frequency, we must release outdated patterns of fear, scarcity, and distraction. Awareness leads to transformation.

Reindigenization – Returning to ancestral wisdom means living in balance with nature, honoring reciprocity, and rejecting colonial distortions of culture.

Oneness & The Illusion of Separation – Science and spirit affirm our deep interconnectedness. The divine moves through all life forms, not solely through humanity.

Artisan's Hands: Shaping Reality – Our hands are extensions of spirit. What we create, nurture, and touch becomes a reflection of our heart's intent.

The Warrior's Path – Centered warriors persuade through truth, honor, and action, not force. Strength is cultivated through discipline and integrity.

Polarity of Creation & Destruction – We are always creating or destroying. Conscious living requires us to choose what we build and where we invest energy.

Ethical Change – Change is not forced but embodied. We align with divine orchestration rather than imposing will.

Wholeness of Spirit – Love, as God loves, is only achieved in a state of fullness. A depleted spirit must be replenished through breath, integrity, and self-awareness.

Reflect & Apply Worksheet

1. Self-Reflection:

What does being centered mean to you?

In what areas of life do you feel pulled away from your center?

How can you cultivate stillness in your daily life?

2. Awareness & Action:

What thought patterns or behaviors keep you trapped in cycles of depletion?

Where in your life can you replace destruction with conscious creation?

How can you honor your breath as a spiritual tool?

3. Connection to Ancestral Wisdom:

What practices from your ancestors or indigenous traditions resonate with you?

How can you integrate nature-based wisdom into your daily rhythm?

What does reindigenization mean to you on a personal level?

4. The Power of Hands:

How do your hands reflect the work of your heart?

What have your hands built, healed, or held that has shaped your path?

In what ways can you use your hands more intentionally?

5. Living in Alignment:

What does ethical change look like in your life?

How can you embody transformation rather than force it?

What small daily habits bring you closer to wholeness?

Lesson XIII: Respecting the Spirit of Nature

"The forest has always been my teacher in peace, in diversity, in democracy. Diverse life forms, small and large, moving and immobile, above ground and below, with wings, feet, or leaves, find their place in the forest." — Vandana Shiva

To walk in harmony with nature is to understand that we are not separate. We are woven into a great web of life, a single thread in the fractal fabric of existence. The ancients knew this, as do the trees, rivers, winds, and mycelium pulsing beneath the forest floor.

To honor nature is to honor ourselves. To protect the land is to protect the sanctity of our own being. When we align with the rhythm of the Earth, we move in accordance with the great design, the codes embedded in creation.

Modern civilization has sought to sever this connection, replacing ritual with routine, reverence with industry, wisdom with profit. The forests – our sacred mothers, our teachers – are felled in the name of progress, their voices silenced beneath the weight of machinery. But the way remains. The way knows.

The universe speaks in patterns, repeating in spirals, sequences, and sacred symmetry. The Fibonacci spiral we see in sunflowers, pinecones, galaxies, and nautilus shells is the same blueprint that shapes our very DNA.

Indigenous tribes of the Amazon understand this, mapping the stars by the same geometric patterns found in Ayahuasca visions. The Dogon people of Mali held knowledge of the spiraling paths of Sirius B before modern telescopes confirmed. Celtic druids wove sacred geometry into their knots, knowing that all things mirror one another. To see these patterns is to witness the handwriting of the cosmos.

The Lakota prophecy warns of a time when humans will become so dependent on machines that they will forget the sound of the wind, the pulse of the Earth, the wisdom in silence. Hopi elders teach: *"One day, you will hear the Earth cry. Her rivers will dry, her animals will fade, and the machines will not save you. Only then will you remember the old ways."*

To live only through technology, industry, and artificial intelligence is to fall into a slumber of forgetting. When we put the machines to sleep, we awaken the ancient knowledge that still lives in our bones. The Haudenosaunee (Iroquois) people practice the *Honorable Harvest*, a principle that teaches us to take only what we need and to always give back to the land.

Robin Wall Kimmerer, an Anishinaabe botanist and author of *Braiding Sweetgrass*, explains: *"Never take the first plant you see. Never take the last. Take only what you need and use everything you take. Ask permission. Give gratitude. Give back. Sustain the ones who sustain you, and the Earth will last forever."* To harvest without reverence is to rob future generations. To take without offering gratitude is to break the sacred agreement between human and Earth.

Modern civilization has spread the illusion that humans are the highest form of intelligence, that the Earth is ours to dominate. This is the greatest myth ever sold. The fungi beneath our feet have been networking and communicating for over a billion years, transferring nutrients across vast forests, sustaining entire ecosystems. Trees speak to one another. Whales grieve their dead. Elephants return to the bones of their ancestors.

In Lakota tradition, the phrase *"Mitákuye Oyás'iŋ"* means *"All my relations."* This is a recognition that we are not rulers, but kin, no greater than the wind, no lesser than the stars. The Amazon rainforest is known as the lungs of the Earth, but the ancients knew this vast expanse of ecosystems as *a living library*, a unique consciousness.

The Celts believed trees were portals to other realms, each species carrying different wisdom. The Bodhi tree beneath which Buddha attained enlightenment symbolizes the interconnectedness of all life. Even modern science now affirms what Indigenous tribes have always known – trees communicate, share resources, and nurture their young. They do not compete – they collaborate. If we are to survive as a species, we must learn from them.

The wind is older than all other languages. Navajo people believe that wind carries whispers from their ancestors, shaping the land, shaping us. The breath of the Earth is our breath, and when we still ourselves enough to listen, we are taught how to move, when to surrender, when to rise.

The wetlands and mangroves are known as the Kidneys of the Earth, purifying the water, filtering toxins, restoring balance. Yet, they are being drained, poisoned, paved over. When the kidneys fail, the body collapses. When the wetlands disappear, so does the lifeblood of the planet. To respect nature is to listen to her organs, to honor her breath, to protect her sacred body as we do our own.

In many cultures, the serpent represents both death and rebirth, poison and cure. The ancient Maya saw the feathered serpent, *Quetzalcoatl*, as a divine bridge between heaven and Earth. Kundalini energy in yogic philosophy describes a serpent coiled at the base of the spine, awakening the seeker to cosmic awareness. Nature, like love, exists in duality – creation and destruction, fire that burns but also illuminates.

To walk in balance is to honor both. To respect nature is to remember that we are not above, but within. To move with awareness, with gratitude, with reciprocity is to walk in harmony with the Earth. The way knows. May we listen. May we honor. May we remember.

Fractals of Abundance

Fractals – seemingly infinite patterns repeating in smaller scales, woven into the architecture of existence. They contrive the clouds, etch their motif into the veins of leaves. Each flash of lightning tessellates the sky, rivers carve their currents with these sacred designs. The spirals of trees, sutures of shells, the aperture of existence – all adorned with the same markings, the signature of the eternal. A myriad of endless affluences births a plethora of unceasing prosperity.

This is how I perceive energy – the voltage animating our cells, the electrons that elevate our frequency, the unseen rhythm pulsing through all things. Despite this, we are burdened by the illusion of scarcity – fear whispers that we will run out, that what we need to exist is fleeting.

What is finite is not necessary for our sustainment. Breath is life. Air is π (Pi), immeasurable, infinite, unceasing. Our bodies keep reserves of fats, proteins, salts, and water, but oxygen is stored nowhere – this life force must be ceaselessly received, a gift the lungs never hoard, a promise the cosmos never breaks. We inhale the biocomponents of the wind, exhale them back into eternity. This exchange is interminable.

The sun beams upon the earth, feeding life without hesitation. Biophoton energy spills into ripening fruit, into blooming flowers, into the roots of trees stretching toward the sky. We drink from the pristine spring, a taste as familiar as a lover's lips. We return for more – and there is still plenty.

Acts of generosity spark a causal sequence, a ripple, inspiring others to give. A compliment. A word of encouragement. A meal for the hungry. A smile that lingers. We scoop from abundance, and yet, abundance remains. There is always enough. There has always been enough.

Put the Machines to Sleep: Honoring the Spirit of Nature

Throughout history, civilizations have risen and fallen based on their relationship with the land. The Indigenous peoples of the Earth understand a fundamental truth: nature is not an obstacle to be conquered, but a living entity to be honored. When we forget this, we descend into imbalance, severing ourselves from the rhythms that sustain all life. The modern world has placed machines above spirit, industry above harmony, and consumption above reverence. But there is a way back.

Earth is crying for balance. We have reached a point where the voices of the rivers, trees, and skies have grown faint beneath the roar of machinery. The forests are thinning, soil is eroding, oceans are suffocating, and the creatures that once roamed freely are now penned, hunted, or extinct. The world is in distress – not by accident, but by design.

Humanity has placed profit over purity, convenience over consciousness, and industry over integrity. In the name of progress, we have built factories that choke the sky, systems that poison the water, and markets that exploit the very beings we share this planet with. The price of these choices is not only measured in environmental collapse, but in spiritual starvation.

Yet, wisdom tells us that the story is not over. Destruction is only one side of the coin – creation remains an option. The time has come to put the machines to sleep and awaken the spirit of nature once more. We must return to natural rhythms.

There was a time when our ancestors knew how to listen. They knew the language of the wind, the songs of the rivers, and whispers of trees. They understood that the land does not belong to us, but we belong to the land. This is the wisdom we must reclaim. To put the machines to sleep is not simply about shutting down industry. This requires shifting our mindset. This involves rebalancing our existence, so that what we build does not come at the cost of what gives us life.

We are required to:

End the worship of excess. The modern world has convinced us that more is better, that success is defined by accumulation. But true wealth is found in balance, in sustainability, in knowing when to give back more than we take.

Honor the natural world. The forests do not need our machines; they need our respect. The animals do not need our industries; they need our guardianship. The Earth does not need saving, we simply need to stop inflicting harm.

Cleanse our consumption. The foods we eat, the materials we use, the energy we expend – these are not neutral choices. Every decision either nourishes or depletes the planet. The time has come to choose nourishment.

Dismantle false power. Systems of exploitation are not strength; they are sickness. True leadership does not extract but sustains. True power does not dominate, but nurtures. The age of control must end so the age of collaboration can begin.

Let the fires that were ignited for corporate growth be extinguished for the expansion of tribes and community. Let chainsaws be silenced, factory farms dismantled, and toxic industries be put to rest. May awareness multiply with haste, so that we do not awaken too late. May we protect the clean waters that remain and purify what has been tainted. Let us not mourn what has been lost but fight for what can still be saved.

Our children deserve skies unclouded by industry, rivers that run wild and clean, forests that whisper the stories of the ancients. They deserve a world where the air is fresh, food is pure, and the spirit of Earth is honored.

Let us cleanse the land, the mind, and the heart. Let us lay the machines to rest and return to the wisdom that has always been waiting for us. The time is now. The way is known.

Forest Kinship: The Ancient Teachers of the Wild

For decades, this forest has been my sanctuary, my confidante, my teacher. She has absorbed my tears, held my secrets, and weathered the release of energies that no longer served me. In moments of uncertainty, I surrendered my fears at her feet, and she paid me back with courage. When I offered her my doubts, frustrations, and pain, she transmuted them into confidence, tranquility, and healing.

I bathed in her waterfall, allowing her sacred waters to cleanse my body and spirit. I knelt beside her roots, pressing my hands into her soil, whispering prayers of gratitude, and asking if she would share her wisdom with me. Each time, she answered – not in words, but in the rustling of leaves, in the hush of the wind through her branches, in the song of her rivers as they carried away all that no longer belonged.

She has taught me the rhythm of life, the ebb and flow of existence, and the sacred art of listening. There is no place where I have ever felt safer. When I run her trails, I close my eyes, allowing my senses to guide me. I know the way not by sight, but by the texture of the earth beneath my feet, by the scent of the ferns, by the voices of the ravens that greet me like old friends. Their wings beat above me, filling my heart with calmness, their calls mocking me, teaching me not to take life too seriously.

She has been a refuge in times of turmoil, a steady presence when the world outside felt uncertain. Beneath her canopy, I have filled notebooks with my thoughts, written words that only she will ever hear. She has never judged, never corrected – only listened. In that silence, she healed me.

I have also known the sorrow of losing her. When the loggers came, when the chainsaws roared and the trees began to fall, I felt the earth tremble. I heard the cries of the birds as their homes crashed to the ground. I watched as my friends, the trees I had leaned against, the ones who had sheltered me, were severed from the mycelial threads that connected them to all that lives. I kissed every stump, held prayers for their spirits, and cried for days.

My stomach has never been the same since witnessing such desecration. The sickness of humanity weighs heavy on the land. How can we call ourselves evolved when we tear apart the very source of life? I demanded answers. I wanted justice.

The forest, in her wisdom, told me to let go. To mourn, but not to be consumed by rage. She reminded me that destruction and renewal are two sides of the same breath. She whispered that she would rise again, as she always has. That I, too, must learn to grow through what has been taken.

This forest has been my greatest teacher – the only preacher I have ever needed. She does not mislead, does not distort truth, does not demand obedience. She simply is. She teaches by example, by presence, by resilience. In her silence, I have found the answers I once sought elsewhere.

If we wish to honor her, we must not merely admire her beauty; we must protect her existence. We must fight for the trees, for the rivers, for the creatures who make their home among the roots. We must recognize that we are not separate from her. What is done to the forest is done to us. May we never forget that we belong to the land, not the other way around. May we walk gently, listen deeply, and inherit the wisdom only the wild can teach.

Trees hold the codes we need to remember what sovereignty means. They are ancient record keepers, standing tall in silent reverence, transmitting wisdom that has been lost through indoctrination, distorted by artificial constructs, and erased by the dissonance of modernity. To those who listen, they whisper the forgotten truths of the Earth, offering guidance encoded in their rings, roots, and branches.

Science has only begun to scratch the surface of what the ancients have always known – nature speaks in frequencies, patterns, and transmissions that extend beyond our limited perception. Neutrinos, subatomic particles that travel through the cosmos and pass through everything, are carriers of information. These tiny messengers move through trees, water, air, and even our bodies, delivering cosmic intelligence that influences our very being. Every moment, we are bathed in a stream of neutrinos carrying data from distant stars, the sun, and the galactic center.

Trees, with their vast networks and deep roots, act as living antennae, absorbing and storing these energetic codes. When we engage with them intentionally, we tap into this ever-present wisdom. Trees are always transmitting, always listening, always available to share their wisdom with those who approach with reverence.

These are ways to tap into the ancient wisdom of trees and access their codes:

Tree Meditation and Consciousness Exchange

Find an old-growth tree that calls to you. Place your forehead against his trunk, close your eyes, and slow your breath. Imagine releasing all thoughts, worries, and distractions. Let your consciousness dissolve into the being of the tree. With each inhale, absorb the wisdom stored within his rings. With each exhale, surrender all that no longer serves you. Stay present, listen beyond the mind, and trust what comes. The tree will speak in sensations, images, or subtle impressions.

Observing Tree Movement and Sound

Watch how trees move with the wind – how they bend but do not break. They teach us resilience and grace. Listen to the rustling of leaves, the creaking of bark, the subtle hum of their existence. There is music in their stillness, messages hidden in their rhythms.

Root Connection: Grounding Exercise

Stand barefoot beside a tree, place your hands on her bark, and visualize your energy merging with her roots. Imagine drawing up her ancient stability, absorbing her deep connection to the Earth. Let your own energy settle, mirroring the tree's patience and strength.

Offering and Receiving Energy

Trees willingly transmute heavy energy. If you are feeling overwhelmed, embrace a tree and silently ask her to assist in recalibrating your vibration. Express gratitude as you receive her stability and calmness.

A tree transmutation is the sacred act of offering all chaos, doubt, fear, insecurity, stress, and uncertainty to an old-growth giant in exchange for calmness, peace, and clarity. Trees do not hold lower vibrations; they elevate them. They operate at frequencies too high for stagnation, too pure for dissonance.

When we align with trees, they adjust us to their level, increasing our voltage and resetting our energy. There is a game we can all play, one where every participant wins. There is no competition, no hierarchy, only the call to embody our truest selves. The rules are simple – be good, be kind, be present. A tree does not compare herself to another tree. She does not seek to overshadow, dominate, or destroy. She simply grows, reaches for light, and offers shelter to those in need.

The trees invite us to do the same – to stand firm in our essence, to grow without resistance, to receive and transmit wisdom with clarity. If we honor their codes, listen with our whole being, and remember their teachings, we will find ourselves aligned with the true nature of existence. They are waiting. They have always been waiting. Now is your time to listen.

Wisdom from Wind: The Breath of Nature's Spirit

The wind is a messenger, a guide, a force that carries wisdom beyond words. She moves freely in all directions, never bound, never stagnant, always shifting with purpose. Those who listen can hear her teachings woven into every gust, every whisper, every mighty storm. She blankets us with her presence, unseen yet undeniable, reminding us that nature's spirit is ever-present, flowing through us, lifting us, guiding us home.

The wisdom carried by the wind – *Windsdom* – is a sacred language revealed to those who take the time to feel her movements, to witness her artistry in the swaying of trees, the rustling of ferns, the dance of pine needles upon redwood branches. Though she is intangible, she makes herself known through the world she touches. She is the unseen made visible, the force that stirs life into motion.

The wind does not cling to one place, nor does she resist change. She reminds us that to remain in flow, we, too, must not allow ourselves to become stagnant in thought or action. The breath of the Earth does not linger where not needed – this force moves, shifts, and transforms, encouraging us to do the same.

Wind spirits are masters of energy, of movement, of balance. They move effortlessly between gentle and fierce, teaching us that both softness and strength are necessary. They know when to be a whisper and when to be a gale, just as we must learn when to be still and when to rise.

When we are stuck in patterns of doubt, hesitation, or fear, the wind reminds us to keep moving.

When we are burdened with stagnant energy, she comes to cleanse us, to refresh our spirit, to stir our souls into action.

When we are deep in prayer, she carries our words to where they need to be heard.

When we are lost, she redirects us, nudging us toward the path we had forgotten.

The wind is a wizard of unseen realms, an ancient traveler who knows no borders. She teaches us that transformation is not something to resist but to embrace. Like the wind, we must learn to flow with change, to move gracefully through uncertainty, to trust that every gust is leading us somewhere purposeful. The wind speaks to those who are willing to listen.

Here are ways to align with her presence and receive her guidance:

Wind Meditation and Breath Alignment

Stand in an open space where you can feel the wind on your skin. Close your eyes and breathe deeply, aligning your breath with her rhythm. With each inhale, receive her wisdom. With each exhale, release what no longer serves you. Imagine your intentions being carried into the universe, knowing that she is taking them exactly where they need to go.

Observing the Wind's Movements

Watch how she interacts with the world – how she dances through the trees, how she plays upon the surface of water. Notice her patterns, her changes in intensity, and ask yourself: What is she teaching me in this moment?

Offering Your Thoughts to the Wind

When you feel burdened, speak your thoughts into the wind and trust that she will carry them away, transmuting heaviness into lightness. When you are grateful, whisper thanks to her, knowing she delivers messages to the great spirit of Earth.

Moving Like the Wind

Be fluid in your journey, embracing change rather than resisting. Let go of rigid attachments and allow yourself to be guided by intuition, just as the wind follows the natural flow of the Earth. Trust that your path, like the wind's, is always unfolding exactly as intended.

The wind does not question where she is going or resist the unknown. Trust her path. She simply moves, carried by an intelligence greater than the mind can grasp. She reminds us that transformation is the nature of existence, not something to fear.

So, be like the wind. Move with grace. Move with strength. Move with trust. Know that your prayers are being carried exactly where your intentions are calling. Dance through uncertainty. Surrender to metamorphosis and change. Feel the wind upon your skin and know that she is whispering: *You are free.*

Kidneys of Earth: Vital Connection of Nature and Humanity

Wetlands are kidneys of the Earth. They cleanse and recharge water, filter pollutants and sediments, and ensure life downstream can thrive. Across the world, these natural filtration systems are being drained, destroyed, or mismanaged to the point where they can no longer function. In America, over half of the wetlands are gone. The consequences ripple far beyond the landscape.

As wetlands deteriorate, we also witness a sharp rise in kidney malfunction and disease in human populations. This is karma in circulation, a reflection of how deeply interconnected we are with the health of the planet. When we diminish the biodiversity of Earth, we deplete the vitality of humanity. The suffering of nature is the suffering of all who depend on her.

Earth and the human body mirror one another. Every organ in our system has a counterpart in the natural world. Just as wetlands act as the kidneys, purifying and regulating, forests act as the lungs, generating oxygen and cleansing the air. Rivers and streams flow as the circulatory system, carrying nutrients and life to all corners of the land. The soil, rich with microbial intelligence, serves as the gut, absorbing, digesting, and replenishing what sustains life.

Each biome on Earth mirrors an organ in the human body:

The wetlands (kidneys) cleanse and purify.

The rivers (blood vessels) circulate vital energy and nutrients.

The forests (lungs) breathe life into the planet, exchanging oxygen and carbon dioxide with every inhale and exhale.

The mycelial networks (nervous system) connect and communicate beneath the surface, ensuring life flourishes in harmony.

The mountains (bones) stand as ancient pillars, providing structure and stability.

When these systems are neglected or exploited, sickness follows. Deforestation suffocates the planet; just as polluted air diminishes lung capacity in humans. The loss of clean water disrupts the body's ability to detoxify. The degradation of soil leads to weakened immune function, as the nutrients necessary for health are stripped away.

As we take from nature without replenishing, we erode not only the land but the foundation of our own well-being. When we desecrate these life-giving systems, we suffer in return – lungs filled with pollution, bodies burdened by toxins, nervous systems overstimulated. To heal Earth is to heal ourselves.

With the loss of biodiversity comes the diminishing of cultural diversity. The health of a land is intertwined with the traditions, languages, and wisdom of those who have stewarded the sacred grounds for generations.

Indigenous cultures, deeply connected to the rhythms of the Earth, have long understood that to harm nature is to harm the people. Where biodiversity flourishes, so does the richness of human culture. Where lost, we see not only ecological devastation but the erosion of knowledge systems, the extinction of languages, and the fragmentation of once-thriving communities.

To conserve nature requires that we save languages, preserve traditions, and resuscitate forbidden knowledge – not only that we protect ecosystems. The wisdom of the elders, the stories of the land, and the ceremonies that honor the balance of life must be upheld alongside the forests, rivers, and wetlands they are tied to.

To restore balance, we must:

Protect the Wetlands – Recognize their sacred role in filtering and replenishing life.

Revive Indigenous Wisdom – Honor and implement the teachings of those who have lived in harmony with the Earth for millennia.

Replenish the Soil – Support regenerative agriculture that nourishes both the land and the body.

Cleanse Our Waters – Advocate for policies and practices that prioritize clean, life-giving water.

Strengthen Our Own Bodies – Detoxify through whole foods, clean air, and pure water, aligning our health with the vitality of the planet.

As we awaken to the undeniable connection between Earth's health and our own, we step into the responsibility of guardianship. Nature does not belong to us; we belong to her. In honoring her balance, we reclaim our own. The time to heal is now. The way is known.

Snake Medicine: Transforming Fear into Sacred Connection

We are conditioned to acquaint ourselves with fear, yet safety is our birthright. Our nature is to be held, loved, and nurtured – not to shrink away from the unknown, but to embrace life in fullness.

Snakes have long been misunderstood, cast into the shadows of myth and superstition. Yet they are among the most vital teachers in the natural world. They remind us that transformation is inevitable, that to grow, we must shed what no longer serves us. Their medicine is one of rebirth, adaptability, and trust in the great unfolding of life.

Since childhood, we are told what to fear – darkness, failure, the wild creatures that slither and crawl. We are taught that snakes are to be avoided, that they are symbols of danger rather than wisdom. But what if we were misled? What if, instead of recoiling, we moved with reverence? What if we saw all beings as integral to the ecosystem of life?

We are instructed to welcome discomfort by casting shadows over what *the teachers* will never understand. We choose instead to shine light on what we require to become whole. They keep us small by directing us to fear what holds them back. We decide to grow when we release all that pulls us from our center. They warn us against what moves without sound, yet in silence we know wisdom is born. We find our strength in stillness.

There is tenderness in trust and sweetness in surrender. The snake does not resist her shedding; she allows, knowing this is part of her evolution. She fully embodies her power, moving fearlessly with both strength and grace.

To hold a snake is to understand the paradox of power and gentleness. She wraps her delicate body around our neck, gives us a taste of her strength, and then consoles and comforts us with her grace. She teaches us that true power is not in domination, but in presence. That strength is not found in resistance, but in flow.

When we move with reverence, we form sacred relations with all life forms. Every creature, every plant, every gust of wind has a place in the great design of existence. Fearing something is often misunderstood. To judge without knowing is to remain ignorant of the wisdom held.

Snake medicine calls us to:

Release outdated fears – What we fear often holds the key to our transformation.

Embrace change as necessary and sacred – Like the snake shedding her skin, we know that growth requires letting go.

Move with fluidity – Rigidity leads to suffering; adaptability leads to freedom.

Respect all beings – Nothing in nature exists without purpose; reverence restores balance.

There is strong medicine in a snake's embrace. She does not take, she teaches. She does not threaten, she reminds. She does not resist, she flows. May we learn from her. May we move like her. May we honor her presence, just as we honor all life. For when we cease to fear the wild, we remember that we, too, are related.

The Honorable Harvest

What if we are here not merely to exist, but to improve the quality of life on Earth? What if our purpose is to be caretakers, to protect the species we share this land with, to nurture the forests, waters, and soil that sustain us? What kind of world would we create if we learned from trees instead of cutting them down? What if we honored the wisdom on land instead of extracting without reverence? The *Honorable Harvest*, as understood by the keepers of ancient traditions, is a sacred agreement – an ethic of taking only what is needed, never more, and giving back in gratitude.

This way of living in harmony, trusts that Earth provides when we walk with humility, care, and reciprocity. Yet, with all the advancements in technology and transportation, people still go hungry, and the land is still used for destructive agricultural practices. A society disconnected from the spirit of nature falls into an imbalance.

As I walk through the forests, I can feel the absence of what once was. Bird songs are quieter. Trees do not dance as they once did. The pulse of the wild has been dulled by human interference. How do we bring back what has been lost? How do we restore the life force that has vanished from the land and within ourselves?

This book serves as a guide, a vessel to remind us of what we already know deep within. Let this be a call to resurrect the love that has always been deeply rooted in mankind – the love that nourishes, protects, and regenerates life rather than depleting. The messages within these pages aim to rescue cultures, save forests, regenerate health, enrich the soil, and revive a planet in peril.

When we stop buying what keeps us oppressed, we begin to purchase our liberation. The greatest lesson I have inherited through writing *The Way Knows* is to always stand for what I know in my heart is pure. I hope you, too, will use these lessons to embrace a healthier way of living and to care for the Earth that nourishes us with seeds of compassion, grace, hope, love, and truth.

May we coexist with all beings who share this land with us. May the goodness of mankind blossom from the shadows cast over our potential. May we move as the rivers move – freely, flowing, and in harmony with the grand design.

Together, we will plant seeds of change, ensuring that the beauty of this world flourishes for the next seven generations and beyond.

Key Takeaways from Lesson XIII

To walk with nature is not a metaphor, but a lived experience – one that restores balance, reverence, and remembrance. We are within, not above nature. Our disconnection from the Earth is the root of much of our collective suffering, and reconnection is the only path forward.

Nature is a living consciousness, not a resource. Forests, rivers, winds, and animals are not passive scenery, but teachers, allies, and sacred kin. Ancient traditions across the world understood this and practiced reciprocity, reverence, and restraint – embodied through teachings like the Honorable Harvest and rituals of gratitude.

Modern industry, technology, and disembodied systems have created an illusion of separation, but the **Earth continues to whisper in her own language** – through trees, wind, animals, and fractal patterns – that the way still knows. We must put the machines to sleep, both physically and mentally, and return to the rhythm of the wild.

Trees are record keepers. Wind is a messenger. Wetlands are kidneys of the Earth. **Everything in nature corresponds to something within us.** When we harm these systems, we harm ourselves, but when we listen, when we give back, when we move with humility and care – we restore both the land and the soul.

To live in harmony with the Earth is a return to wholeness, not an act of sacrifice. The call now is not just to survive, but to reawaken the sacred bond we were born to uphold.

Reflect & Apply Worksheet

1. Self-Inquiry: Reawakening Connection

Where in my life have, I forgotten the sacredness of nature?

When did I last truly listen to the wind, trees, silence?

What is one memory I hold of feeling connected to the land?

2. Personal Practices for Reconnection

Reflect on which of the following you feel called to begin or deepen:

Tree meditation or grounding practice.

Listening to the wind as sacred transmission.

Giving thanks before harvesting food or resources.

Offering something back to Earth (prayer, water, compost).

Visiting a natural sanctuary for silence, listening, and presence.

3. Integrating Ancient Wisdom into Modern Life

What teachings from Indigenous cultures, elders, or nature-based wisdom resonate most with me?

How can I apply the Honorable Harvest in my consumption?

Where am I still unconsciously contributing to harm (overconsumption, waste)? What shift can I make today?

4. Rewriting the Story

How does nature reflect parts of myself I have neglected?

In what ways can I become an active guardian of Earth?

What kind of world do I want future generations to inherit – and what role will I play in shaping this?

5. Commitment to the Sacred Path

Complete these sentences from your heart:

"I honor the Earth by…"

"The way I choose to walk forward with nature is…"

Author's Epilogue: Becoming a Vessel for the Way

The way has always known. Moving through the seen and unseen, weaving rhythms through breath, through thought, through every unfolding moment of existence. This is the pulse beneath our feet, the wisdom encoded in the stars, the force that whispers when we quiet our minds enough to listen.

To become a vessel for the way is not to conquer, or to command, but to surrender to celestial orchestration, to allow divinity to flow through us unimpeded, to walk in harmony with the currents of existence. We embody the way when we stand still in a world of noise, to hold purity in a world of pollution, to cultivate presence when distractions beckon us away from our center. We return home – not to a physical place, but to the stillness within where the way has always resided.

The great masters of old taught us that truth is not something we chase, but something we allow to move through us.

Lao Tzu said, *"Stop thinking, and end your problems."* Stillness reveals the path. The river does not ask where to go, the pull of gravity is simply followed. When we let go of resistance, we, too, are carried out exactly where we need to be.

Yeshua taught, *"The kingdom of God is within you."* There is nothing to seek outside ourselves. To find the way, we must clear the obstructions, strip away the illusions, and return to the sacred knowing that has always lived within us.

Buddha spoke of non-attachment, *of how suffering arises when we try to hold onto things that are meant to move.* Love, wisdom, and purpose do not thrive under grasping hands; they flourish in an open palm, in the space where faith meets surrender.

Through this book, you have walked the realms of mastering self, aligning with divine orchestration, living in integrity, committing to love, and unifying with spirit. You have expanded your understanding of discipline, cultivated reverence for nature, and explored the depths of living in alignment with the sacred.

You have explored the discipline of the mind, the sacredness of breath, fluidity of the body, and intelligence of the microbiome. You have learned that the way is not an external path to be found, but an inner knowing to be remembered. The way is a force of nature, as ancient as the stars, moving through all things and guiding those who choose to listen.

To be a vessel for the way is to embody integrity, to move with reverence, to become an instrument of divine will. We learn to:

Stay out of our own way – We release self-sabotage, addictions, and the illusion of control. Do not obstruct the flow of divine wisdom with the clutter of the mind.

Trust divine orchestration – All is unfolding exactly as intended, and resistance only delays what is already destined. Have faith in the timing of the universe.

Commit as a loyal lover – We are honoring devotion, transparency, and the sacred responsibility of love. Love is not possession; love is alignment with another soul's highest good.

Show your children a good way – We lead by example, embodying the wisdom we wish to pass on. They do not learn from our words but from the energy we carry.

Respect the spirit of nature – Knowing we are not separate from Earth, but part of her intricate design. Forests breathe wisdom, rivers whisper direction, and wind carries prayers.

The bacteria within your gut, mycelium beneath your feet, and breath moving through your lungs – all of existence reflect this truth: everything is interconnected. What is done to one is done to all. The pain of the Earth is reflected in the sickness of man. The restoration of the land is mirrored in the healing of the soul.

To walk the way is to trust this connection, to know that purity keeps us aligned, stillness keeps us centered, and love keeps us whole. You will forget, at times, as all beings do. The world will pull, distractions will call, doubts will creep in, but the way does not disappear. The way knows. When we listen, so do we.

One Day

One day, our world will unite. People of all lands, colors, and stories will gather, not in conflict, but in communion. The illusion of separation will fade like mist in the morning sun, and humanity will awaken to our true nature – interwoven, indivisible, whole.

Religious walls will dissolve, replaced by reverence for the sacred in all things. No faith will war with another, for we will have remembered that divinity speaks in many tongues yet sings one song. No one will be cast aside based on the way they pray, or whether they pray at all. We will come to know that love is the only true creed.

Wars will become relics of a past we no longer glorify. Instead of conquest, we will cultivate harmony. Nations will not be drawn by borders, but by the collective desire to nurture and uplift. The battlefields will turn to gardens, and hands that once built weapons will shape homes, heal the wounded, and tend the land with care. The scars of separation will heal, leaving only the wisdom of what was learned.

One day, all children will be safe. No child will go to sleep hungry, wondering if they will see another sunrise. No mother will shed silent tears, fearing she cannot provide. The laughter of the young will echo freely, unburdened by war, by neglect, by displacement. Fathers will be present. Families will be whole. Lineages will be strong, not just in blood, but in the love that binds generations together.

One day, humanity will cease to exploit the Earth. We will recognize the folly of extracting wealth from lands that were never ours to take. The hunger for gold, oil, and diamonds will be replaced by the hunger for wisdom, connection, and balance. No longer will forests be felled for profit, nor rivers poisoned for industry. The rainforests will breathe again, undisturbed, as jaguars, toucans, and tribes of the old world reclaim their sacred homes. The oceans will glisten free of plastic, and the creatures of the deep will no longer fear the shadow of man. The Earth will heal, and with her, so shall we.

One day, our understanding of wealth will shift. We will discover gold – not in the mines of distant lands, but in the depths of our own minds. We will cease to measure abundance by accumulation, but rather by what we give, what we create, and what we leave behind for those yet to come. We will build legacies of kindness, empires of generosity, civilizations of peace.

One day, the frequency of our galaxy will reach an unsurpassed high. Our thoughts will no longer be bound by fear but will soar with vision and purpose. We will embrace the infinite potential that has always been within us, harnessing energy not for destruction, but for evolution. Technology will be guided by wisdom, not greed. Science and spirit will no longer be at odds, but in sacred dance, revealing the great design that has always been.

One day, we will look back at this era and see the turning point – the moment when we choose a new way. When we let go of the chains of division and rise, not as individuals, not as nations, but as one people, one world, one light.

This begins now. With you. With me. With all of us being guided by *The Way*.

Note to My Children: A Legacy of Wisdom

My Sweet Children,

I want you to know that faeries really do exist. That which you seek is already seeking you. There are angels in awe of your golden glow. Your imagination is a bridge to what is real, not a place of fantasy. The world beyond the screen is where life unfolds in truth; what you dream, you manifest, and what you create shapes reality.

Your heart exudes purity, your love runs deeper than the oceans and seas – mightier than galloping horses, more powerful than stampeding elephants, stronger than the wildest river currents. Your worth is greater than the last number ever counted.

You are woven from the same light as the stars, and your soul carries the wisdom of ancestors who walked this Earth long before you. You are children of the cosmos, forces of goodness, beacons of joy, and guardians of truth.

You are loved. You are admired. You are appreciated. You are adored. I will protect you. I will fight for you. I will be the father I once longed for as a child. Thank you for choosing me.

As your father, my greatest mission is to embody the guide I always needed, to offer you the strength of my spirit, the protection of my love, and the wisdom I have gathered on this path. The road to bringing us together was not without hardship, yet through years of persistence, resilience, and unwavering faith, I accomplished what once seemed unattainable.

When we are together, I am whole. You remind me that harmony is not found in external pursuits but in the sacred moments we share. Walking barefoot through forests, feeling the sacred embrace of ancient trees, running with the waves as they greet the shore – this is life.

We build. We climb trees. We play guitar. We read. We sing. We learn. We prepare plant-based meals with love, nurturing not only our bodies but our spirits. Every moment I have with you is a treasure, and I honor our time shared fully.

I want you to always know the importance of connecting with nature, of listening to the trees, of honoring the language of the wind, of respecting the wisdom carried in the rivers and mountains. Treat all life with gentleness and reverence. You are part of something vast and sacred, woven into the great design of existence.

May you remain untouched by the wicked ways of engineered culture, never losing your sense of wonder, never forgetting the magic of the world around you. Let your imagination roam freely. Let your heart remain pure. Let your spirit stand unshaken in the presence of those who have forgotten how to dream. The world may try to pull you away from your essence but never let them take the light from your eyes. Never allow your song to be silenced. Never permit your wild, beautiful soul to be tamed.

There will be moments when the path seems uncertain, when the world's noise grows too loud, when doubt creeps in like a shadow. In these moments, return to your breath. Find your center. Remember who you are.

You carry within you the strength of all who came before you, the wisdom of the Earth, and the light of creation. You were never meant to simply exist – you were meant to expand, to love, to shine.

Know that no matter where life takes you, you will always have a home within my heart. You will always have a place to return to, arms ready to hold you, a voice to remind you of your worth, and a spirit that walks beside you, unseen but unwavering.

Nobody will ever love anyone the way I love you. My heart bows in humility and gratitude to be your father. You are beautiful, brilliant, kind, fun, wise, and radiant beyond measure. You are my greatest gifts.

Know that I will always be here, walking beside you, protecting the light within you, reminding you of the wisdom already written in your bones.

With love eternal,

Your Dad

About the Author

Jesse Jacoby is a dedicated father, expressionist, and advocate for compassion, equanimity, and purity. He expends energy adventuring in forests, creating, learning, playing, and writing.

Jesse is the founder and CEO of Soulspire: The Healing Playground (*soulspire.com*). This is a biohacking and purification center with locations near Lake Tahoe in Truckee, CA, and in Nevada City, CA.

He is also the founder of the Global School of Purification (*schoolofpurity.com*), which is an educational course instructing how to regenerate health in the body and providing certifications for global purification specialists.

Jesse is the author of The Raw Cure: Healing Beyond Medicine (1st & 2nd Editions), The Way Knows: Trusting Divine Orchestration, Where Galaxies Kiss the Earth, Gaia Speaks, Eating Plant-Based: The New Health Paradigm, Society's Anonymous, and My Quest to Conquer What Matters.

His acoustic album, titled Light Night of the Soul, will be released in 2025.

Jesse@soulspire.com